D0978221

"Harkness is the epitome of the difference between knowledge and wisdom. She is able to distill volumes of information into useful, practical advice. I am delighted that she has made the effort to share this wisdom through her books."

Irvin C. Shambaugh, president,
Aptitude Inventory Measurement Service (AIMS)

"Helen Harkness saved my life! After a twenty-plus-year career ended, I found myself 'wandering aimlessly' trying—unsuccessfully—to find my niche. I could never have succeeded had Helen not come into my life and helped me pave the right path."

Ed Bamberger, CEO, The Single Gourmet of Dallas-Forth Worth, Inc.

"This book eloquently and in very practical terms shows us how to embrace chaos as a tool of change. Let Helen Harkness deliver you from angst and confusion and guide you to a new, more positive perspective that offers both reality and hope. A wonderful book."

Rex McGee, screenwriter and member of
the Writers Guild of America and Dramatists Guild

"*Capitalizing on Career Chaos* is a perceptive guide for making sense of the changes affecting work and careers. The author's wit, insight, and practical advice make it a certain winner. A must-read for individuals seeking to manage their careers and for career counselors and coaches."

Keith O. Nave, president, Career Management
Partners/Lincolnshire International

"Harkness has led many of us to new directions in our careers. In this book she expands on the concepts she has taught for years and updates them for today's fast-changing environment. A must-read for everyone facing career or personal challenges."

Buddy Frazer, owner, MPF Services; chairman,
Dallas County Historical Commission

"Helen Harkness is a legend in career counseling. Whether you're a disgruntled lawyer, unhappy executive, unsatisfied academic, or frustrated technologist, she can help you change your career and your life—for the better."

"The author's approach to writing, like her approach in dealing with her clients, is practical and available to put to immediate use. An invaluable tool in making the most of a change of career scenery."

"Helen Harkness brings experience, focus, and practicality to the career counseling process. I was grateful for her guidance as I made a major career adjustment, and twenty-five years later I still recommend her to others."

"A wise and wonderful guide through the world of career chaos. Whether you are a midlife career changer like me or someone who is looking for a sane, reassuring voice in the mass of career advice, this book can move you from fear to new career."

"Helen Harkness's approach to career planning in this era of relentless change has rescued many of us from the dark abyss of an unhappy, misguided work life. Her message about embracing change is important not only to individuals considering career shifts, but also to business leaders who understand the value of people who are passionate about their work and fearless in the face of chaos."

CAPITALIZING on career CHAOS

Bringing Creativity and Purpose to Your Work and Life

HELEN HARKNESS

Davies-Black Publishing
Mountain View, California

Published by Davies-Black Publishing, a division of CPP, Inc., 1055 Joaquin Road, Suite 200, Mountain View, CA 94043; 800-624-1765.

Special discounts on bulk quantities of Davies-Black books are available to corporations, professional associations, and other organizations. For details, contact the Director of Marketing and Sales at Davies-Black Publishing; 650-691-9123; fax 650-623-9271.

Cover illustration: Michael Rowley/Stockart.com

Visit the Davies-Black Publishing Web site at www.daviesblack.com.

09 08 07 06 05   10 9 8 7 6 5 4 3 2 1
Printed in the United States of America

Library of Congress Cataloging-in-Publication Data
Harkness, Helen
    Capitalizing on career chaos : bringing creativity and purpose to your work and life / Helen Harkness.— 1st ed.
        p. cm.
Includes bibliographical references and index.
    ISBN 0-89106-209-2 (pbk.)
    1. Career changes. 2. Career development. 3. Creative ability. 4. Crisis management. 5. Quality of work life. I. Title.
HF5384.H3695 2005
650.1—dc22

                                                                2005004529

FIRST EDITION
First printing 2005

CONTENTS

ACTIVITIES

PREFACE

No problem can be solved from the same
level of consciousness that created it.

—ALBERT EINSTEIN

Careers are the lens through which I view the world. Enhancing careers in chaos and in conflict with former dreams and expectations has been the focus of my work for three decades. I am a teacher and strategist and when it comes to capitalizing, not capsizing, on career chaos, I have been there personally and professionally. Crisis and disorder ultimately brought purpose and creativity to my life and work.

I frequently take a moment to thank my maker for the chaos in my early forties that forced me to refocus my career direction, to move positively forward through the very real pain of change in my life and work, and to gain the meaning and purpose for pursuing my personal power. I later realized that in changing my career I was ahead of my time—that in the future it would become a more normal course of events for adults. How on target I was!

Since my doctoral study focusing on careers and the incorporation of my company, Career Design Associates, in 1978, I have relentlessly studied past, current, and future forces affecting and transforming the workplace: the economy, the business world, the educational system, technology, society, and the individual. I have coupled this active research base and my extensive experience with adults and their careers with the intuition and foresight gained from my life/work experiences.

It is paradoxical that what provided me with insight and direction in the midst of confusion and chaos thirty years ago came not from my humanities education but from a totally random contact with the newly emerging science of chaos and complexity. It's almost as if I became overloaded and an entirely different approach was necessary. Understand, however, that this book is career focused and not a scientific treatment of the theories of chaos and complexity (though I can provide a bibliography and probably own most of the publications of the major contributors to the field of quantum physics). It is an exploration—a search for what we nonscientists can learn from this developing science. My purpose is to communicate what I have learned from my research and my personal and professional experience—with its checkerboard of successes and failures—that might provide insight, guidance, and direction to adults seeking to take creative control of their careers in this uncertain age. Discovering that chaos breeds creativity (by breaking apart the known and familiar) was what I have since labeled a personal power point, keeping me moving forward at a time when all carefully laid plans had turned to mush!

I remember well my introduction to Alvin Toffler and future thinking in 1970. I was sincerely, if rather ineptly, trying to keep bored freshmen awake in a Monday-Wednesday-Friday 1 p.m. English class. Giving up on Shakespeare and the glories of the Elizabethan Age and striving to be relevant (the rallying cry of the seventies), I dashed out and almost instinctively—since I had read only a short review—bought a stack of Toffler's *Future Shock*. The book was selling briskly (sales would eventually top 7 million copies—an unbelievable number since it didn't revolve around Hollywood, sex, quick-fix motivation, or a get-rich-quick formula). And it gave us a new term, "future shock," which entered our vocabulary and frankly now describes much of our current life.

I can't say how the book affected my students, but it triggered a powerful, life-changing "Aha!" of critical insight for me. This was the beginning of my focus on change and the future—the writing, research, speaking, and teaching; the establishment of Career Design Associates, Inc.; my active career consulting at the World

Future Society conferences for two decades; and publication of three books: *Best Jobs for the Future*, *The Career Chase*, and *Don't Stop the Career Clock*.

In the early 1970s, Toffler's prediction of three to five career changes seemed ludicrous until I thought more deeply. Up to that point hard work and a college degree had been touted as the magic keys—all that one really needed for career success. Couple this with the reality that in the early 1970s only one in nine Ph.D.s found a teaching position in academia; vast numbers were driving taxis and teaching part-time in junior colleges with a salary that, when all the extra time was added up, amounted to minimum wage. Gypsy scholars were in and tenure was out!

As a physician's wife in the 1960s, I had read that if a woman got a Ph.D., she could possibly become president of a university. Ten years later, I had to face the realization that as a single parent, I could not rear three children on the salary I earned as a teacher/administrator at a small liberal arts college that was on the verge of closing. I also could not expect to teach at a first-rate university because of the fifteen years I had taken off to spend with my children. I recognized that with a Ph.D. and a dime, I could get a cup of coffee. After some thought, brought to the surface by Toffler's forecast, I knew that a career change was my destiny.

Toffler's definition of future shock described my life at that time: total disorientation, shattering stress, and overwhelming unexpected change, parachuting me into a chaotic world where reality clashed with my former expectations and rules. Identifying that I was indeed in future shock released me from the negative search to attempt to identify the mistakes and failures I assumed I had made to create all these problems for myself.

It was amazing how this insight changed my perspective, set me on a positive course, and settled me on my purpose in life. My quest became the search for understanding and focus in my life by studying careers, the change process, and the future. For thirty years my purpose, pursued with passion and persistence, has been to translate my insight into effective strategies to teach adults how to gain creative control of their careers in this chaotic, confusing, and changing work world.

The future, as forecast, has arrived. Changing, recharging, refocusing, renewing, recareering, and multicareering are only now being seen as a necessity for career success and not the indulgent, irresponsible actions of an immature, indecisive person! This, combined with the mass of change from all directions, shows that we are indeed experiencing Toffler's future shock.

So, where are we today? And what's next? We are immersed in an important cultural transition—continual change and uncertainty are our reality. From necessity or desire we must embrace a new way to define and handle our careers.

Though a nonscientist, I have gained much from chaos and complexity theory. Primarily, I have learned that chaos and complexity are not simply negative confusion breaking up our world. They are the mechanisms through which change is initiated and organized, the first steps by which the world creates diversity, rebirth, and renewal. Chaos is everywhere: Mastering chaos for our career success requires new ways of seeing, thinking, and acting. This is what I teach my clients in career transition and what I would like you, the reader, to realize and use.

Instead of being orderly, stable, and in equilibrium, as expected from our past, our reality is seething and bubbling with change, disorder, and process. However, our system of thinking has forced order over it—*made it fit* and ignored all information that didn't seem to belong. Disorder has been treated as negative noise to be avoided at all costs. However, all systems have subsystems that are continually fluctuating, and at times a combination of these will become so powerful that they reach a bifurcation point, a branching or forking, that shatters our preexisting organization. This can be a huge catastrophe or merely a fringe event. It is impossible to predict which direction change will take—whether the system will become chaotic, from which a higher order spontaneously arises through a process of self-organization, or be a barely noticeable ripple.

We individuals—human beings—are self-organizing systems capable of creating a higher order out of chaos in a chaotic world, and we can no longer wait for the majority, our authorities and institutions, to lead the way as they did in the past. The great physicist Erwin Schrödinger said that it takes at least fifty years—half a century!—for a major scientific discovery to penetrate the public consciousness. We cannot afford this! The cost is too great to our ecological systems, career relationships, health, culture, and collective future. We are duty-bound to search, question, and open our minds. Pioneering is becoming an increasingly psychospiritual venture, since our physical frontiers are all but exhausted.

I've found that institutions—schools, government, and churches—rather than providing leadership and direction in helping us deal with future shock and unrelenting change, frequently trail at least a decade behind. For the most part they are doing what they have always done, and often in the same old way. As a result, many established systems no longer meet our critical needs. Yet we continue to count on them with apparently little awareness of the gap between what is being provided and the reality of our needs.

It is clear to me now that all the uncertainty, chaos, and triggering events I experienced forced me to cultivate and release my creativity, resilience, commitment, and indeed the cornerstones of my resourcefulness and strength. I have written this book to bring order to my thinking about chaos and careers, since order and chaos exist side by side. I must understand and assimilate the knowledge if I am to move to the next step in my growth and development. For my career clients, I must integrate and communicate my insight and information on these very deep changes that carry danger and opportunity. Where I have been on this subject for years feels to me like the essential warm-up time of an orchestra, all instruments sounding on their own, tuning up individually but together unmelodious and discordant, with no recognizable tune. Before I move forward in my work, I want to write the score, hear it played, and pass it on to others. As a teacher, I am dedicated to passing on career-related insights. Bringing coherence to my thought process relating careers and theories of chaos and complexity is critical for me to move forward and make my next leap of learning.

ACKNOWLEDGMENTS

A special appreciation

To my clients, from whom I learn much and who trust me to be committed to do whatever is effective, legal, and ethical to help them achieve their purpose—and I expect them to do the same for themselves and others! To my former clients, who have graciously and thoughtfully shared their career insights and information with current clients. To my professional colleagues, from whom I gain much insight, and whose well-being and good fortune I value. And to Dr. John Holland, whose research and tools have been especially meaningful in my career work with adults.

To my grandchildren, Laura, Lucas, Leslie, Bonnie, and Milo, and my daughters, Jane and Ann. When I expressed the concern that my grandchildren, because of my schedule and geographic location, would not remember me as a cookie-making grandmother, one spoke up: "Not a cookie maker but a money maker! Calories are out—a car and college beats cookies anytime!" This may be the emerging paradigm for contemporary grandmothers.

To my sister, Madolyn Stewart, who has traveled with a limited budget and made friends on five continents, and who, though chronologically older, serves as a role model for me and my clients on how to stay young in spirit—and deserves credit for carrying much of my personal load, as well as hundreds of books to and from our library.

To the Reverend Willie Cobbs, whose weekday role is caring for my greenhouse plants and our newly developing Oak Tree Farm. He is patient with my passion for plant growth because, as he explains it, "It's in your heart and you can't help it!"

A very special thanks to Robert Kraakevik, reference librarian at the South Garland Branch of the Nicholson Memorial Library. Since the staff is a library's most important asset, Bob—who changed from a career as a teacher/businessman at midlife—has demonstrated how valuable one in his position and with his commitment can be to the community.

To Shelley Fleming; without her (and Scotch tape, scissors, and erasers), this book would not have become a tangible reality. Shelley successfully and patiently read my notes, corrected, suggested, edited, and researched online. I am deeply grateful for the order she can magically create from my manuscript notes.

And finally to Lee Langhammer Law, Laura Simonds, and Connie Kallback at Davies-Black for their professionalism, responsiveness, attention, encouragement, energy, and patience!

ABOUT THE AUTHOR

Helen Harkness, Ph.D., is a pioneer in career management who founded Career Design Associates, Inc. (CDA), in the Dallas–Ft. Worth area in 1978. Her work through CDA reflects and integrates her multidimensional career as a successful entrepreneur in business and investments; an experienced educator and administrator (former academic dean/provost, college professor, and director of continuing education); and a director of human resources and human services in city government.

A superb strategist and resourceful catalyst, as well as an experienced teacher, futurist, consultant, researcher, and speaker, Harkness spurs others to act while providing resources and realistic direction for the process of change. Harkness's CDA credo and battle cry in today's uncertainty is: "Freedom is knowing your options." With her CDA clients, she founded the Pathfinders for the Future Think Tank, which meets monthly to explore, research, and forecast current trends and future possibilities as they relate to the workplace. This has created 400 videos and DVDs on specific careers for client use. Harkness has also written and produced a series of educational videotapes, *Careers in Finance* and *Discovering Career Options*, featuring John Holland, author of the *Self-Directed Search* assessment; and, through CDA, has created the Internet Career Design Assessment Profile™, a career assessment process for individuals in the workplace. Harkness teaches classes on careers through Southern Methodist University and The S'Cool, a privately owned continuing education company.

Regularly quoted in newspapers and magazines across the country, Harkness is author of *Best Jobs for the Future* (1996), *The Career*

Chase (1997), and *Don't Stop the Career Clock* (1999). In 2003, she received the first Professional of the Year Award from the Association of Career Professionals (ACP International), Dallas–Ft. Worth Chapter. The award permanently carries her name as the Helen Harkness Professional of the Year Award.

Helen Harkness, Ph.D.
Career Design Associates, Inc.
2818 South Country Club Road
Garland, Texas 75043
phone: (972) 278-4701 fax: (972) 278-7092
options@career-design.com
www.career-design.com

INTRODUCTION

The work world is up for reinvention in so many ways. Creativity is born in the reinvention . . . . We can't wait for great visions from great people, for they are in short supply at the end of history. It is up to us to light our small fires in the darkness.

—CHARLES HANDY

In this era of rapid change and uncertainty, our conventional, traditional career planning for success is archaic—as outdated as the slide rule or the typewriter. The customary paths to career success—the linear corporate (go to college, get a job, move up the ladder and stay for forty years, retire to die!) and the steady-state path of the professional specialist (the doctor, lawyer, teacher, or engineer)—are absolutely over. Today the average career will likely include two or three occupations and multiple employers. Millions will spend time in self-employment, and 12 to 27 million will be in microbusinesses with four or fewer employees (Peters 2003, p. 239). The spiral career path with significant changes about every seven to ten years—nontraditional and somewhat frowned upon in the past—is rapidly becoming the necessary new norm.

The necessity to unlearn our former career concepts and to change and redirect our careers, perhaps multiple times, is a growing reality. Though predicted by futurists for more than three decades, this reality is only now reaching center stage for most Americans. The new model is unbelievably difficult for adults reared, perhaps unconsciously, to expect and revere a predictable, linear journey based on stability and certainty, consisting of twelve to twenty years of schooling, followed by a forty-year career path, and then, typically, total retirement.

It would be foolish to predict the exact shape of careers in the future or to suggest a quick fix to the current career crisis facing many adults as career expectations collide with reality. What is needed instead is an awareness that the current crises create both danger and opportunity for career growth and development, and an understanding of how that awareness can be used to capitalize creatively on the chaos of change. The purpose of this book is to provide career-related information, insight, strategies, connections, and encouragement for adults to gain their personal power, freedom from fear of change, and an understanding of their options.

Working successfully now and in the future demands that we assume direct responsibility and control over our individual careers. This will require insight, creativity, and an action plan based on a different perception—a new way of seeing and experiencing the reality of our evolving, changing culture, ourselves, and the working environment.

The critical issue is how we as individuals can live and work in our age of constant change and chaos, making a successful transition from the Industrial Age to the age of technology and innovation, and still achieve the personal and career goals that we value. Resolving this issue involves creating a shift in our identity and establishing a new conceptual framework.

Because in this country we are tied so closely to the work we do, some very real changes in our self-concept, our definition of who we are, need to be made. For many, this can be frightening and even paralyzing. To be a truly functioning person we must have a sense of identity—a sense of our place in the environment. This is wholeness—uniting that which we perceive ourselves to be and that which we perceive others to see and to expect of us.

We are currently experiencing problems in work identity because the reinforcement messages received from our workplace and society, and perhaps from our own selves, are scrambled and fragmented instead of being strong and supportive. For this reason, it is critical that we have the confidence, courage, and competence to think for ourselves: to reexamine our expectations, attitudes, behaviors, decision-making processes, and perceptions of career/self reality, as well as to become aware of the external changing realities in our environment. How congruent are all our former, accepted rules with what is really happening in our work world in this first decade of the twenty-first century? Are we really on track to achieve what has meaning for our work lives, or are we sidetracked on a fast track to nowhere? Are we, like Alice, speaking to the Cheshire Cat?

> "Would you tell me, please, which way I ought to walk from here?"
> "That depends a good deal on where you want to get to," said the Cat.
> "I don't much care where," said Alice.
> "Then it doesn't matter which way you walk," said the Cat.
> (Carroll 1946, p. 62)

We must know where we want to go. We can't wait for the world, our traditional institutions, our culture, our social and educational systems, to catch up with us and our career problems and map out exactly how to solve them. We must solve these ourselves, but not *by ourselves*. To succeed we must connect, communicate, and collaborate with others. We must take the calculated—but educated and informed—risk of jumping into our best future.

We also need to develop a distinctively new conceptual framework of thinking about our career problems and issues that will give us a sense of continuity between our past, present, and future experiences. This is the essential foundation for developing clear, harmonious life/work goals and a plan for achieving them. Trying to solve problems in the same old way is like continuing to look for a lost object in the same drawer. The following preview of the chapters in this book will give you a sense of how we'll approach the broad topic of capitalizing on career chaos.

Chapter 1, Understanding Chaos for Career Planning, focuses on the big picture—the deeper environmental shifts and thinking about how our contemporary world works. Beginning in the 1970s, chaos and complexity theories, which demonstrate the capacity of living systems to respond to disorder (nonequilibrium) with renewed life, have become cultural metaphors. Our reality is rapidly moving from simplicity, stability, and certainty to complexity, instability, and unpredictability. Our current decade is experiencing extreme chaos created by this transition. It is critical that we individuals who are being thrust out on the cutting edge of change recognize that chaos creates the birth of new opportunities.

Part I, Living and Working on the Edge of Chaos, discusses a new career pattern that is rapidly evolving, replacing our revered vertical forty-year-certainty career ladder (Chapter 2); the search for the authentic self (Chapter 3); and the experience referred to as "the dark night of change" (Chapter 4).

Part II, Redesigning Our Careers, provides details of the career design process. These include looking inward through a variety of self-assessment processes to gain authentic awareness (Chapter 5); looking outward for information about the challenge, needs, and opportunities in the external world (Chapter 6); looking forward—coordinating the internal and the external into a coherent future vision (Chapter 7); and taking action to reach our goals (Chapter 8). In Chapter 9, we will take a brief look beyond the individual to chaos and change in organizations.

ONE

Understanding Chaos for Career Planning

All the tumult and seeming chaos, when viewed in the light of historical perspective, can be seen to represent not only the death agonies of an older order but also the birth pangs of a new epoch—a new golden age which assuredly will outshine those of the past.

—L. S. STAVRIANOS, HISTORIAN

Over the past few decades, chaos theory has been used widely in the natural sciences. More recently, it has begun to be applied to the social sciences as well. Understanding the key characteristics of chaos theory (and the related theory on complexity) leads to a shift in how we view change and an understanding of our ability to influence and use change creatively.

The Advent of Chaos

Edward Lorenz was a research meteorologist and mathematician working at the Massachusetts Institute of Technology in the early 1960s. His job was coming up with accurate forecasts and weather models to help meteorologists, and it was beginning to seem futile. His weather models forecast the same weather day after day, yet the weather outside changed constantly. On this particular day, Lorenz as usual started the next run of data on his now-antique computer and trekked down to the coffee-pot to avoid the noise. When he returned to his desk, he found that instead of spitting out the expected and usual patterns, the weather pattern predictions were fluctuating wildly.

Lorenz was really puzzled; his intuition told him that something significant was happening. But as he retraced his actions just before leaving the room, he found that nothing was different. He'd done everything just as he'd done it a hundred times before. Then he remembered: He had abbreviated one of the numbers he was using to represent atmospheric conditions. Instead of entering 0.506127, he had rounded the number to 0.506 and, after entering it, left the program to run. What he discovered on his return—that a very small difference (less than one part in one thousand) in the initial conditions led to large changes in the weather predicted by his model over time—developed into what we know today as chaos theory and revolutionized the way we think about change.

We are moving into an age that will require an active imagination and an ability to change dramatically—not abilities we have traditionally cultivated. There are no separate, isolated problems anymore. We are all tied together in a system, and when we move one part, all are affected. If we want to gain any real insight into our personal and career problems, we must connect those problems with the broader changes and shifts in our world.

The step-by-step planning of the career models of the past is obsolete. Career planning today acknowledges and even embraces the messiness of social, economic, demographic, and political phenomena and their often unexpected events. It requires insight into how and when to change and when to adapt or discard old patterns while retaining essential elements to incorporate into new patterns.

ORDER OUT OF CHAOS

The threat of terrorism and the economic downturn in the early 2000s could be termed unexpected wild cards, but they demonstrate the unpredictability of our world. In the 1990s, stability in good jobs seemed a certainty, and companies were in competition for talented people. We can learn from our own career chaos and the radically varying messages we receive that disorder can evolve from order quickly and unexpectedly, and also that order can be just around the corner from chaos. In reality, order and chaos travel together.

Recognizing that chaos has its roots in order and can actually be the source of creativity can help you develop a different perspective on your life and your career. It can help you understand and begin to capitalize on the seemingly random, unpredictable changes constantly bursting uninvited into your world.

Ilya Prigogine, a Belgian physical chemist, received the Nobel Prize in 1977 for his work on the thermodynamics of nonequilibrium systems and specifically for the theory of dissipative structures. Prigogine was investigating chaos as a scientist, but his work served as a springboard to more philosophical concerns: the nature of time, the fate of science, and the destiny of human life.

According to Prigogine, dissipative structures are in a state of nonequilibrium; that is, they are unstable and subject to endless fluctuations. Prigogine found that a *dissipative structure*—any self-organizing, renewing system—could be a person, a chemical solution, a seed, a school system, a city government, a culture, a dynamic pattern in the brain, or anything capable of change and interaction with its environment. Societies have limited powers of integration; Prigogine said that if the perturbations—the initially small changes outside the normal system—exceed the power of integration, the system is destroyed or gives way to a new system or organization. Isn't this happening today on myriad fronts?

As chaos theory implies, order and disorder are mirror images, with disorder as a source of new order. There seems to be a contradiction between the words *dissipative* and *structure*. Dissipative describes a loss, energy ebbing away, but it plays a constructive role in the creation and rebirth of the new. Dissipative-like disorder does not lead to the end, but is the first part of the process from which new forms develop. It makes way for a new structure to be created.

Prigogine insists that order and organization can actually arise spontaneously out of disorder and chaos through a process of self-organization. When changes occur as a result of the relationship between order and disorder in far-from-equilibrium conditions, we find that very small perturbations or fluctuations can become amplified into gigantic, structure-breaking waves. This sheds light on all sorts of qualitative or revolutionary change processes.

After the former structure breaks up, the possible new can grow in its place and take the organism to a higher level. *This rebirth with self-renewal is the essential characteristic of all self-organizing and self-renewing systems.* When you are deeply involved in recovering from the loss of your old career or job focus, you must internalize this important insight.

Unlike machines, human beings are highly self-organizing, self-renewing organisms. The renewal does not occur, however, unless the former model or standard breaks apart. This is where chaos enters. Chaos and the breaking apart of former career goals and expectations can signal the birth or renewal critical for growth. Disorder can be the source of new order. While dissipation describes a loss, energy ebbing away, it does not necessarily lead to demise. Instability can be the key to transformation.

Transition involves relinquishing parts of the past and taking hold of the future. You must determine first what to hold firmly from the past to continue to build on; second, what to turn loose; and third, what new piece to pick up or add on. It's a process of "hold on, drop off, create, and build." It is critical for organizations experiencing cultural change to understand this if they are to remain successful. It is equally critical for adults forced into a recareering process, either by the unavoidable loss of their former career or by an interior psychological shift that dictates the career change.

CHARACTERISTICS OF CHAOS

A few characteristics of chaos deserve review before we move ahead.

Unpredictability

Where once all was orderly and predictable in our careers, now there is confusion and complexity—downsizing, offshoring, bankruptcy, and terrorism. Perturbations and shifts that originally appeared small, incidental, and random, hardly worthy of notice, suddenly loom as major disorder, creating changes quite different from those anticipated at the starting point: a geographic move, a new manager, a medical report, a merger, new insight into self, situation, or others.

Unpredictability is one of the primary elements of chaos. Small unpredictable shifts can eventually create great change. This "butterfly effect"—from the title of a 1979 paper by Lorenz called "Predictability: Does the Flap of a Butterfly's Wings in Brazil Set Off a Tornado in Texas?"—drew little attention for about ten years. The idea is that in a chaotic system, small disturbances grow exponentially, rendering long-term prediction impossible. When the initial conditions begin to change in chaotic behavior, the difference, though quite small, can increase rapidly, leading to dramatically different pictures of the same process. In other words, when we are seemingly in a stable state, changes now labeled weak signals (that start out as barely noticeable or identifiable) can very quickly expand. We must keep our foresight and intuition open to what could be possible.

Complexity

Another concept closely linked to chaos is *complexity*. With many interconnecting points, *complex adaptive systems* make up most of our social world of people, politics, and commerce. Complex adaptive systems include the world economy, human language, an individual, whole societies of people, school systems, nations, companies, solar systems, ecologies, spiral galaxies, lumps of coal, rain forests, the human brain, colonies of ants, mushrooms, tadpoles, and so on. Just about anything that can be recognized and discussed is a vast complex adaptive system with many interconnecting points.

No complex adaptive system exists in isolation. Even lumps of coal absorb heat from the environment and radiate it back when they cool off. They are adaptive and have the ability to process and incorporate new information and change or respond to new information, to which they are sensitive through a process of adaptation—capable of individual and cooperative action. Complex adaptive systems don't just respond passively to change, but turn it to their advantage to improve their situation. Several characteristics are worth noting. Complex adaptive systems

1. are self-organizing and learn from the environment, using input and output exchange of information with the environment

2. adapt and change as a result of positive and negative feedback loops

3. depend on and incorporate a constant flow of new information into old patterns

4. are capable of regeneration, self-renewal, learning, developing, and growing

Nonlinearity

Chaos theory developed as scientists began to see and understand the dynamics at work behind the seemingly random behavior of nonlinear systems. Through their research and the use of powerful computer models, scientists have demonstrated that beneath the seemingly chaotic behavior of a nonlinear system there is order—a type of self-organizing pattern, shape, or structure.

As a result, the rules of behavior have been turned upside down: Order appears in chaos. Randomness has a kind of predictability within its own paradoxical *laws of chaos,* which reveal a hidden order and predictability in apparent disorder. They are irregular in the short run, but predictable in the long run.

Simple *nonlinearity*, an important characteristic of complex adaptive systems, can behave in extremely complicated ways. Most natural and social dynamics are nonlinear. The linear process—do this, this, and this, and the result will be a predictable outcome—does not hold with human nature. In our human affairs in everyday life we learn that a tiny event over here can have a major impact over there. Nonlinear systems are not locked permanently into previously learned but obsolete ways. They welcome and require creativity and intuitive thinking.

Creating your work space by integrating your personalized work style, strengths, and business instincts requires nonlinear thinking. Accepting nonlinear thinking opens the door and welcomes creativity and intuitive thinking—an absolute must for our career success today. No longer can we expect to use a rigid time-tested formula or either/or, black-and-white thinking and action in order to understand our world or move forward in it.

Emergence

Emergence is a concept that relates to the creation of a whole new system developed by joining together separate pieces. This process creates synergy—cooperative, collaborative teamwork—but also an independent and individualistic effect. Emergence is the unintentional production of what becomes a whole new system of global patterns of behavior created by separate agents in a complex system cooperatively joining together and interacting according to their own local and independent rules of behavior. These global patterns cannot be predicted from the local rules of behavior that produce them. They arise from the bottom up.

M. M. Waldrop (1992, p. 200) describes emergence as creating a sense of barriers spontaneously crumbling, letting loose new ideas—a kind of open-ended freedom that demonstrates synergism and that the whole is greater than the sum of the parts.

NAVIGATING CAREER CHAOS

To redefine a career identity when the familiar one is no longer possible, desirable, or satisfying, adults must become change conscious, future oriented, and precedent breaking. These are highly challenging tasks for those thoroughly trained to be rather passive, good followers, who have long valued and expected stability and security, and who have honored all past traditions.

Paradigm Shifting

Taking a holistic creative approach to solving complex human-related problems is the major theme of this book. To succeed today we must rethink our work-related rules, myths, and expectations, and then design and build a new career model for ourselves based on our current internal and external realities. Because the old career model isn't working as it did originally, a paradigm shift—a new way of thinking about old problems—is needed.

This new paradigm will include some older or partial truths while allowing optional ways of working. The new paradigm transforms our traditional knowledge and rules while reconciling apparent differences. The new framework predicts more accurately and opens up new areas of explanation. Embracing the new requires letting go of the old by understanding the phenomenon we are dealing with. We can learn to foster healthy change without the paralyzing fear of crisis. We can ask questions in a new way—reframe them in a different context.

In 1996, consultant Joel Barker created a training film titled *Discovering the Future: The Business of Paradigms*. He describes a paradigm as a set of rules that define our boundaries and act as a filter for our view of the world, influencing our perceptions and judgments. He defines a paradigm shift as "surprising, abrupt, unprecedented, revolutionary rules altering change." To use his terms, if we have "paradigm paralysis," a terminal disease of certainty, as opposed to "paradigm flexibility," we will not succeed when we are at the edge of chaos. Barker notes the following major paradigm shifts that altered the basic rules of society in the twenty years from 1966 to 1986: "From pollution to environmental protection, cheap energy to energy conservation, big automobiles to gas-saving economy cars, copper wire communications to fiber optics and satellites, the role of minorities, computers, medical technology, a woman's place—these changes broke rules that we assumed were the only ways to do things."

Duane Elgin, author of *Promise Ahead* (2000), stresses that each time humanity's paradigm has changed, all life has changed with it, including our work, the way we live, how we relate to each other and how we see our role in our society and its place in the universe. He explains that a paradigm is our way of looking at and thinking about ourselves and all around us. It sets our limits, the emotions we feel, and the reality we perceive. It structures our basic way of seeing, thinking, valuing, and doing with our perception of reality. It tells most of us what's important, what's real, and what's not. "It's our window to the world and it shapes how we see and understand the nature of reality, our sense of self and our feeling of social connection and purpose" (p. 45). It goes to the core of people's lives, changes our view of reality and can be felt in the body, heart, mind, and soul. Paradigms operate beneath the surface of popular culture, unnoticed until the old way begins to generate more problems than it solves. Table 1 illustrates the some of the major paradigm shifts in science. Table 2 illustrates some of the paradigm shifts that will be needed to be successful in a career today.

According to Elgin (2000, p. 43), the trend that "could transform our impending crash into a spectacular bounce is a shift in our shared view of the universe—from thinking of it as dead to experiencing it as alive." This lets us experience ourselves as alive—ultimately connected and related to all—cousins to everything in a living, continuously regenerated universe. This is a different way of relating to our world, and it overcomes the profound separation and division of everything into parts that has marked our past. These shifts in perception may seem so subtle as to be of no consequence.

Table 1: Science Paradigm Shift from Certainty to Complexity

OLD SCIENCE Newtonian Reductionism 17th–19th Century	NEW SCIENCE Relativity, quantum physics, Chaos/Complexity 20th Century–Present
Clock metaphor	Computer metaphor
Mechanistic machine model	Complex adaptive system—seed model
Linear	Nonlinear
Precision	Spontaneity
Equilibrium: producing nothing	Nonequilibrium: creating renewal
Static, stable	Dynamic, turbulent
Reductionism—partial (parts)	Holistic—synthesis
Order, stagnation, symmetry	Disorder, chaos, anarchy
Predictable	Unpredictable, "butterfly effect"
Dualism—"either/or"	Multi—"both/and"
Dissociated, disconnected	Emergence—togetherness, relational
Specialization, determinism	Systems thinking processes
Uniform, deterministic	Random
No change: non-renewal, limited growth	Self-organization: adaptive, exchange between order and disorder
Entropy	Self-renewing, growth
Controlled	Fluctuation
Isolated—separate, unconnected	Independent—connected, relationships, flexible network
Restrict—withhold	Empowerment—permit
Disconnection—nonconnected	Process—strategic thinking
"Power over"	"Power with"
Divide and conquer	Synthesize and "win-win"

Table 2: Career Paradigm Shifts

Old Career Paradigm	New Career Paradigm
One career for life	Multicareer, re-careering
Certainty, determinism	Uncertainty, ambiguity
Analytic, rational	Intuitive, creative
Rigid	Adaptable
Competition, win-lose	Cooperation, collegial, win-win

"Yet all of the deep and lasting revolutions in human development have been generated from just such shifts" (p. 44).

Elgin lists three other times in human experience that our view of reality has been so transformed that it created a revolution in our sense of ourselves, our relationship with others, and our view of the universe. The first transformation in our view of reality and identity happened about 35,000 years ago—the dawn of human culture—in our beginning capacity for reflective consciousness, for "knowing that we know," and the development of early stone tools, cave art, and burial sites. The second transformation occurred roughly 10,000 years ago when humanity shifted from a nomadic to a more agrarian, settled existence in villages and farms, and about 5,000 years ago when city-states began. Our perceptual paradigm transformed for the third time about 300 years ago when our agrarian society shifted to the radical dynamism and materialism of the scientific-industrial era.

We are now in humanity's fourth major shift, which will transform our lives. The paradigm of "old science"—the scientific-industrial era—has brought us great benefits and the forty-year certainty career path, but it is now generating problems that are actually catalysts for a major shift. When Einstein said we can't solve problems at the same level at which they are created, he was describing a paradigm shift. This fourth shift is a convergence of insights from modern science and the world's spiritual traditions. At the heart of this shift is the idea that our cosmos is not a fragmented and lifeless machine, as we were supposed to believe for centuries, but a living organism that is unified, has great energy, and continuously regenerates.

Elgin emphasizes that we have great freedom to act within the limits established by the larger web of life within which we are immersed. No one part determines the functioning of the whole, yet everything is interwoven. A living universe is a learning system in which we are free to make mistakes and to change our minds; since the universe is continuously re-created, we have opportunities and the freedom for fresh starts.

Freedom is at the foundation of our new model. Freedom is knowing that we have career options. Yet at the heart of freedom is uncertainty. Useem (2003, p. 30) describes how people cope in a zone of perpetual anxiety. Danger, real or imagined, can concentrate the mind: A low level of stress typically helps us to focus on the problem, and decision making actually improves. However, when anxiety becomes too great, we become overwhelmed and shut down, and the result is suboptimal decisions.

Kevin Kelly, in *Out of Control* (1994), gives a bit of advice on today's chaotic world: "Seek persistent disequilibrium. Neither consistency nor relentless change will support a creation. A good creation, like good jazz, must balance the stable formula with frequent out-of-kilter notes. Equilibrium is death" (p. 470).

Systems Thinking

Systems thinking is a way of seeing the world as a web of interaction and linkages characterized by a wholeness that is more than the sum of its parts. It can't be understood by analysis of the varying parts, but it can be highly connected across lines and disciplines. For example, the brain has 100 billion neurons—take one out and it still works. No master neuron or central area controls what a neuron does, yet all engage in cooperative behavior.

Paul Finari (2003, p. 28) credits Leonardo da Vinci as the inventor of systems thinking because he recognized, appreciated, and spent his life seeking the connections between all things, phenomena, and processes. For example, he dissected bodies to link the anatomy of muscles to the shape of skin; experimented with light and color to find the connections between what we perceive and illumination; wanted to understand the factors that determined the range of a cannonball or the formation of waves on the sea; searched for the answer to questions such as why seashells were to be found in rocks high in mountains distant from the sea, and why lightning is seen long before the thunder is heard. He demonstrated that creativity could be considered the art of making new links and connections between diverse ideas in widely separated fields. Leonardo da Vinci can inspire and guide creative individuals to greater understanding of the world, greater knowledge of themselves, and subsequently, to greater accomplishments in whatever field of endeavor they wish to master.

Systems thinking is critically important to solving career problems. It allows you to move from seeing the world and your work life in terms of disjointed events to recognizing patterns of connection and interaction in your personal and professional environment. Moreover, it allows you to gain an understanding of the underlying structures that are responsible for generating these patterns. Instead of looking at one thing at a time and noting its behavior, the systems approach looks at a number of different and interacting things and observes behavior as a whole under diverse influences.

Authentic Self-Reference

An *autopoietic structure* is a living system that is self-renewing, autonomous, and with a separate identity yet connecting symbiotically with others. It is adaptable—making choices and changes. It focuses on activities required to maintain its own integrity and self-renewal and to practice punctuated equilibrium for sudden changes based on information. It changes by referring to itself, and every future form it takes will be consistent with its established identity—its *authentic self.*

This autopoietic system is very strong and does not occur in a random way. It demonstrates that the living together of two dissimilar organisms works when the objective is to maintain and re-create itself; changes are not random but consistent and mutually beneficial.

This authentic self-reference is what facilitates orderly change in turbulent environments. Individuals and organizations must have a clear sense of identity—of the values, tradition, aspirations, competencies, and culture that guides them. This is the real source of independence from the environment. When the environment demands a new response, there is a reference point—a center for change. This self-reference prevents an organization from random, self-defeating searches for new customers and projects. With individuals, this genuine self-reference to the authentic self guides the changes they must make.

Meaning Magnets

According to chaos and complexity theories, there is a base of activity within complex adaptive systems that has such a strong magnetic force that it pulls all random behavior toward it and creates a coherent and repetitive pattern. This base of activity is called a *Meaning Magnet.* Meaning Magnets are the end state toward which a dynamic system moves. These attractors have the power to keep the dynamic parts of the system focused and within boundaries. When chaos or disruption occurs, the Meaning Magnet pulls the system toward its pivotal point and facilitates re-creation of its identity. If scientists disturb the system by knocking it away from the behavior, it tends to return to it quickly; the behavior is repetitive (Briggs and Peat 1999, p. 64). Meaning Magnets create consistent patterns that repeat themselves and show that chaotic systems have patterns lurking beneath their seemingly random behavior.

This concept—discovering the basic patterns within random chaos—parallels the process necessary for us to achieve success as we maneuver our careers in today's chaotic workplace. To succeed in today's complexity and chaos, we absolutely must identify our own Meaning Magnets. They relate directly to managing change and uncertainty in our career and workplace.

PART 1

LIVING AND WORKING
ON THE EDGE OF CHAOS

The edge of chaos is where new ideas and innovative genotypes are forever nibbling away at the edge of the status quo and where even the most entrenched old guard will be eventually overthrown.

—M. M. WALDROP

The art of balancing order and chaos is a major talent in today's world. The transition stage between order and chaos is referred to as the *edge of chaos*. This is where we are finding it necessary to balance our worklife today. At the edge of chaos, a system—in this case our career— is paradoxically stable and unstable at the same time. Emergent order occurs when parameters reach critical values, causing the system to operate within or at the edge of chaos. For an individual, creativity and courage are required for an exciting journey into open-ended evolutionary space with no fixed or predetermined destination. The critical issue is this: Using our awareness and insights from chaos/complexity theory as a starting point, how can we capitalize, not capsize, on chaos in our current edge-of-chaos career paradigm? What are the contributions from this new science that we can integrate into our careers? How can we successfully apply chaos/complexity theory to our search for meaning, money, creativity, and coherence?

This edge of chaos is the constantly shifting battle zone. Seeing chaos as a womb, a place of possibility and growth, provides opportunity for creativity, rebirth, and renewal. Being on the edge of chaos means we have to come up with a new way to define, manage, and deal with our lives and careers in the workplace: to reevaluate our direction and define our career success while successfully intertwining stability and instability, certainty and uncertainty, and chaos and order.

Our frame of reference from the past is based on the mechanistic models of Newton and Darwin, which stress that

- victory over rivals equals success

- without a blueprint you will fall into disorder and anarchy

- staying in total control is critical

When the attempt to apply this frame of reference to today's reality doesn't work out over the long term, it provokes depersonalization, cynicism, disillusionment, anxiety, and hostility. Balancing life and work on the edge of chaos will be the continuing challenge both for individuals and their careers and for organizations. Both must recognize and utilize the growing reality of change.

The three chapters in Part I are Finding Our Contemporary Career Paradigm, Searching for the Authentic Self, and Experiencing the Dark Night of Change. In Part II we will apply the principles described in these chapters to a career design plan.

TWO

Finding Our Contemporary Career Patterns

Change is coming, and coming fast. One question confronts every institution and every individual: Fight the change or grab hold and enjoy the ride? I say: Enjoy yourself! It's later than you think.

—TOM PETERS

Our careers, institutions, organizations, and personal lives are vibrating with seemingly out-of-control, random change and transformation. All our expectations based on the past are out of sync with current daily reality. Managing careers effectively and successfully requires a new paradigm for understanding and handling our careers and the work world. Our former stable, predictable, vertical forty-year career model is being replaced—this means living and working on the edge of chaos—paradoxically moving between stability and instability, cooperation and competition, order and disorder, intuition and analysis, certainty and ambiguity.

Mythological Metaphor: Sisyphus Versus Proteus

Sisyphus was the Greek mythical character who displeased the gods and was sentenced to the outskirts of Hades, where he daily pushed a heavy stone up a steep mountain, only to step aside and watch as it rolled back down again. Sisyphus eternally and hopelessly repeated his meaningless task. He saw no options: only the stone and the mountain. The existential, the hopeless, purposeless crisis or irrationality of our work life can be expressed in the myth of Sisyphus.

Proteus was the Greek god who had the gift of prophecy and could change shape when he sensed danger. Robert Lifton (1993), referring to this god, writes that the Protean Self is the "evolving sense of self appropriate to the restlessness and flux of our time. This mode of being differs radically from that of the past, and enables us to engage in continual exploration and personal experiment" (p. 1).

DISCOVERING OUR MEANING MAGNETS

In the midst of the chaos of the change process, just when supposedly all should fall apart, the Meaning Magnet comes into play. Meaning Magnets are seemingly random patterns shaping our lives that give us a real sense of ourselves and life's deeper meaning. Identifying our Meaning Magnets is the first and most important step in taking charge of our career: *discovering what has such a deep meaning and purpose for us that, once identified, it will characterize our behavior.*

As human beings we are complex adaptive systems and are characterized, by nature and design, by an ability to grow, learn, change, adapt, re-create. We don't have to know the exact end and outcome before we start—as long as we know we honor what is true for us— our Meaning Magnets. Meaning Magnets are imbedded and consistent patterns that we consciously or unconsciously repeat. Sometimes we gain insight into our Meaning Magnets through an event, an issue, a memory of a significant accomplishment, or an internal development to which our system is sensitive. It may arrive from our system's percolating information or through emerging conditions that already exist but remain submerged. If our Meaning Magnets are ignored in the long term, we will lose focus on our purpose and meaning in life and work.

Our Meaning Magnets are as unique as our fingerprints. These deeply held patterns can be seen in stories from our life and work. They are woven together by our talent, motivations, values, needs, interests, skills, strengths, and accomplishments that demonstrate them. Margaret Wheatley (1994) refers to them as the essentials that enable us to "wander through the realms of chaos, make decisions about what actions will be consistent with our purpose, and emerge with a discernible pattern or shape to our lives" (p. 136). One's consistent "I," the Meaning Magnet pattern based on instincts, values, and talents, is matched with the current and rapidly emerging changes and opportunities in the work world. The successful combining of dreams and reality, of head and heart, is essential to our career success today.

Tapping into Our Daydreams

Determining a career path and successfully maintaining command of it is not a linear, one-time event nor the step-by-step, vertical career ladder; neither is it neatly packaged like academic courses, with a definite beginning and ending date. It is a continuing complex and creative process of growth. In redesigning our careers, we tap into our dreams and aspirations and deal with the reality of our selves.

According to Dr. John Holland, a creative and commonsense researcher and thinker, and certainly the longtime guru of vocational counseling, "We don't have a random set of daydreams or aspirations" (*Discovering Career Options*, 1987). He recommends that we actively remember our dreams and aspirations and determine their relationship to each other and to the current career. When we trace the elements that tie them together, we may discover the element that is still strong for us, and can be directly related to a missing need in our current work dissatisfaction. This process also helps us to believe, accept, and frame the consistency of our own "I" over time.

Creating New Meaningful Patterns

Once we are aware of our Meaning Magnets, we can forge our own new and meaningful patterns to bring underlying order out of chaos. Highly creative people see below or through obvious layers. They make patterns for new relationships, connecting people and things in new ways. They build frameworks and lay out pieces in unique directions.

Our past is not our potential. We are not permanently trapped by the trained rigidities of our culture that so immobilize us, such as defining success as who dies with the most money—we only seem to be. In reality, we have options and can shape and reshape ourselves into different patterns that fit us and our world as we require or desire.

We can thrive without the rigid success formulas.

Developing a fluidity in our nature permits all kinds of combinations and recombinations of skills, motives, values, and experience. To do so, we must develop the ability to see and find unifying order and coherence in ourselves and in the happenings in our world. We will then be able to give expression to opposite sides of our nature at the same time—conscious and unconscious mind, reason and passion, aesthetic and scientific impulses. To find purpose we can pursue with passion, it is absolutely essential for us to understand, identify, and activate our Meaning Magnets, as they are the major certainty we can count on.

To fully and innovatively use our Meaning Magnets for career success on this edge of chaos, we must identify them based on our authentic self (see Chapter 3). For most adults in today's world, this is a real challenge requiring creative, intuitive, out-of-the-box thinking.

DEVELOPING A TYPE CC PERSONALITY

Expecting career success in the twenty-first century by demonstrating the personality and work traits learned as Industrial Age employees is setting ourselves up for failure and disappointment. We need to begin a process of reinventing and re-creating ourselves.

To thrive in today's chaotic workplace, we cannot retain the highly driven, competitive, frequently mindless Type A personality. Nor can we function with the passive, complacent, usually submissive, laid-back Type B personality, thoughtlessly seeking stability and security at all costs. These two personality types do not have the characteristics to thrive in our evolving edge-of-chaos paradigm. To deal successfully with change, we need to stimulate and release a new personality type that can capitalize on our current uncertainty and complexity. We will call this a *Type CC*, or *change catalyst*, personality.

A catalyst suggests a positive impetus, acting as a stimulus, an activator, a mover, a teacher who can positively spur and trigger growth. The goal of the Type CC personality is to stimulate career growth and renewal on the edge of chaos. Accepting today's reality that careers are in collision, while realizing that grieving over the world as it was "supposed to be" is a waste of time and talent, we need to work on developing traits of the Type CC personality. These traits, shown in Table 3, are necessary to move successfully through all the current career chaos.

Table 3: Type CC Personality Traits and Their Descriptions

Change Catalyst (CC) Personality Trait	Trait Description
Courage and confidence to change	We face fear and forget fear of failure; we focus on freedom to choose options without getting lost in the decision making; we maintain realistic optimism.
Challenge and commitment	We thrive on a learning curve and on overcoming obstacles to meeting goals by accepting uncertainties and balancing the frequently puzzling paradoxes of success and failure, positive and negative.
Creativity and curiosity	We look for "ahas," seeking insight, intuition, and foresight to visualize and explore innovative ways to solve ambiguous problems; we tolerate ambiguity.
Competence and compensation	We can achieve meaning *and* money, doing well while "doing good," maintaining expertise and skills, having a sense of right timing.
Control and cooperation	We can work independently, but also thrive on communicating, collaborating, and connecting with alliances; we must fully realize the value of connections and networks.
Common sense and crap detector	We can be aware of and bypass the tyranny of authority, outdated conventional wisdom, and stale rules for personal and professional success.

THREE

Searching for
the Authentic Self

*Strange is our situation here upon earth. A hundred times every
day I remind myself that my inner and outer lives are based on
the labors of other people, living and dead, and that I must exert
myself in order to give in the same measure as I have received
and am still receiving.*

—ALBERT EINSTEIN

As we pass a store window, we can readily identify ourselves in the
reflected crowd—there's no problem confusing our outward appear-
ance, the external self, with someone else. Yet our individual internal
identity—who we really are—can frequently remain a mystery to us
as well as to others. Even so, when nothing around us feels certain,
our source of certainty must come from within ourselves. This is a
necessity, but we have been conditioned to do the opposite—to look
mainly externally to locate tools for our success. Therefore it is a
challenge for us to look internally. "It is so much easier to deal with
the external world, to spend our lives manipulating material and
institutions and other people instead of dealing with our own souls"
(Palmer 2000, p. 82).

Developing the Type CC personality necessary for the future and
searching for our Meaning Magnets must be based on what we will

call the authentic self. James Masterson (1988) labels this the "real self" and Margaret Wheatley (1994) calls it "self-reference." This is a basic necessity if we are to thrive on the edge of career chaos. To know our authentic self is a highly internal, individual process.

What if we did know, really know, ourselves? What if we identified our strengths and developed them to a high level and, at the same time, understood that too much of a strength can be a weakness and allowed for that? Authentic self-reference and keen awareness of our changing world facilitates orderly change in turbulent environments. To succeed, we must have a clear sense of identity—of our talents, values, traditions, aspirations, competencies, and the culture. This genuine self-reference to the authentic self guides the changes the individual must make. This is the real source of independence from the environment. When the environment demands a new response, there is a reference point—a center for change. This self-reference also saves an organization from random, self-defeating searches for new customers and projects.

AUTHENTIC SELF AS CAREER BASIS

Since a successful career on the edge of chaos must be based first on our authentic self, it is essential to gain insight into its qualities. The concept of the authentic self is holistic and includes the *intrapsychic*—the soul, mind, spiritual aspect, and the unique, individual characteristics of the whole person. Without this personal integration and the insight eventually matched with the opportunities and challenges of the world we live in now and in the near future, careers run a high risk of never being really satisfying or successful.

We must fully tap into and integrate the real self, which Masterson (1988, p. 23) asserts is made up of the sum of the following:

- The intrapsychic—our self-image
- The perceptions of significant others

- Our feelings associated with those images

- Our capacities for action in the environment guided by these images

Psychological struggles confront us all, but only when we are firmly grounded in a strong authentic self can we live and share our lives with others in way that is a healthy, straightforward expression of our deepest needs and desires. In so doing, we can find fulfillment and meaning.

Images of the authentic self come from both reality and fantasy: what we wish as well as what we are. Our authentic self consists of all our self-images, and we can have many—parent, church member, family, partner, community, professional—plus the ability to relate or integrate these to each other, and to recognize them as ultimately forming a unique individual. The authentic self allows us to recognize within ourselves that special someone who persists through space and time, who endures as a unique entity regardless of how the various parts shift and change.

"When you manage a task or relationship well using your own unique style, the experience is integrated to reinforce your self-image" (Masterson 1988, p. 25). This explains why people who have been in non-fitting careers have so little insight into themselves; their work has not reinforced their authentic self. The authentic self carries a conscious awareness of one's essence. According to Doc Childre and Bruce Cryer (2000), "real authenticity is an expression from the core of compassion, understanding and intuition" (p. 107).

Where do people find the courage to live the true self? They must realize that, as Parker Palmer (2000) suggests, "True self is a true friend. One ignores or rejects such friendship only at one's peril" (p. 69). People come to understand that "no punishment anyone might inflict on them could possibly be worse than the punishment they inflict on themselves by conspiring in their own diminishment" (p. 34). The punishment imposed on us for claiming true self-care will never be as damaging as the punishment we impose on ourselves by failing to make that claim. Palmer continues that no reward any-one might give us is greater than the reward that comes from living by our best lights (p. 34).

Our internal identity can be just as evident as our shop-window image, once we begin to search for it. We can do this by assessing ourselves and looking at the internal landscape. To be successful on the edge of chaos, we cannot remain fearful or strangers to our-selves, never really becoming acquainted with who we are behind the mask we intentionally or unintentionally wear. Authenticity is honestly being oneself in relation with others, dropping pretense, defenses, and duplicity—the end of playing it cool or safe or putting a spin on the unauthentic self. Self-disclosure, even to ourselves, requires courage. However, be assured that the payoff of being one-self is a feeling of freedom and comfort, the bedrock of self-confidence and self-esteem.

This is the kind of in-depth self-assessment—the self-knowing—that we must have in order to take charge of our careers in this increasingly turbulent environment where there are few fully func-tioning standard rules for success. This self-reference, as Wheatley (1994, p. 94) labels it, is a clear sense of identity, and our values, traditions, aspirations, competencies, and culture guide this. This clar-ity can be a source of freedom and independence from the environment.

Discovering the authentic self certainly is not an automatic, sim-ple step. Only recently has our society even started to condone look-ing at one's self and internal needs; although, since the time of Sophocles, Plato, and, later, Shakespeare, "Know thyself" has been a commonly repeated credo. Unfortunately, in our culture it can be especially difficult for men to delve into this realm. As one serious, successful young male lamented, "You don't know how hard it is to think through to know and write out what we are really all about! It's like breaking up a concrete block! It's as difficult as learning a new language. I've never done this before."

Under the old career paradigm, there were fairly rigid rules set by our society, our family, and ourselves. As a general rule, we had few questions about who we were or where we were going—either it didn't matter or we somehow already knew it all. We assumed that there was an automatic pilot, or a cruise control, so that we merely positioned ourselves and let it roll! "Know thyself" was not on the flight plan for most of us.

Authenticity will be a key word for career success on the edge of chaos. Under pressure, where many are today, we are not going to take the time or have the inclination to deal with bogus, artificial, conventional nonsense. Alan Cohen (2002) reminds us that the words *authority* and *authentic* come from the same root word, signifying that the root of genuine power is "realness." "Real power is not power over others; it is power to be yourself. Anyone who needs to dominate or defeat others to feel powerful is disconnected from their authentic power. . . . Real power does not compete; it finds a way to synchronize" (p. 16).

Authenticity is being oneself in relations with others, personally and professionally—dropping pretense, defenses, and duplicity—it's the end of detachment. This self-disclosure requires courage, not to be, but *to be known*. Honesty can be a health insurance policy. When we are fearful and succeed in hiding our being from ourselves and others, never matching our self-concept to our possible reality, we lose touch with who we are. This loss of self contributes to illness and problems in myriad forms.

THE FALSE SELF

Each of us must find ways to articulate and bring the inner self into harmony with the outer world. We do this through love and work, as Freud pointed out, by discovering partners or projects that satisfy our needs. Some people, however, can deal only with a narrow slice of life, and in a pathological way. To avoid the fear and depression that would result if the real self did emerge, a false self arises to restructure and make it safe. According to Masterson (1988), the thoughts are "I'll give up searching for my real self and all that would make me truly happy in exchange for never feeling the fear of being alone with my real self or the pain of abandonment" (p. 19).

Masterson believes that the search for meaning in our life and work is the search for expression of one's real self. However, those with an impaired sense of self are frequently unable to find a meaningful fit with their environment. The false self that has been created to deal with their world has no real foundation or bedrock in their authentic self. The false self that many project is not developed to deal with the realities of life as we may assume, but to implement defensive fantasies—not adaptive, but defensive. The false self doesn't seek to master reality, but simply to avoid painful feelings. It induces a lack of self-esteem, and the person quickly settles for rigid, self-destructive behavior that avoids the challenges of life and the accompanying pain, but leads ultimately to feelings of failure, lost hopes, unfulfilled dreams and despair, according to Masterson (1988, p. vii).

Ill at Ease in One's Own Skin

The French refer to these false fronts as "mal a l'aise dans sa peau"—ill at ease in one's own skin. A spirit of trust and openness with self and others is absolutely critical, but not possible if we feel like a fake!

A main element in the career self-assessment process for change is to begin to detach emotionally, at least from the present situation. This requires stepping out of the role and persona we may have simply wandered into or pressured ourselves into assuming, for whatever reasons, and examining and redefining on a deeper level what we are really all about. This period of time with no fixed identity can be a dark, difficult, challenging period. This is not a "check-the-answers," quick-fix, overnight-mail response, but a real pursuit to know ourselves and understand our needs and to connect these with rapidly shifting needs and opportunities in the turbulent external environment. It sounds simple and straightforward, but understanding one's self in order to build continuing meaning and purpose into our life is an emerging and continuing challenge of our age.

Self-Destruction

Many following the false self are caught in a web of self-destructive behavior and can't see a way out. They believe the problems were created somewhere "out there" and fail to see how they themselves created or at least contributed to them. The solutions are out there somewhere: the perfect job, the perfect man or woman, the right diet. People who lack an awareness of their authentic self have a real problem with the process of taking creative control of their career. Their poor coping skills are demonstrated by low self-esteem, lack of self-confidence, alienation, and highly self-critical behavior. Some have unrealistically high expectations of themselves and their possible achievements in the work world, see no way to achieve these goals, and so do not even begin.

When our great expectations crash on external realities, creating a chasm between self and society and between one part of ourselves and another, the stage is set for a sense of loss and aging to invade our thinking, regardless of chronological age. When the work from which we expect a sense of continuing growth and stimulation becomes an obstacle course strewn with lethal mines, or if the edge of a dead-end rut becomes the horizon, we will feel hopelessly trapped.

Depersonalization Feeling trapped can result in depersonalization, a sense of despair common today. The individual no longer recognizes himself as a personality, but he observes his actions as an outside onlooker, feeling deadness, emptiness, apathy, and a sense of monotony. Loss of soul is not only estrangement from oneself, but the entire world is flat (Hillman 1985, pp. 105–107).

Addiction In reality, cynicism, bitterness, depression, depersonalization, anger, and anxiety reflect the way many Americans are handling their uncertainties and lost expectations. Addiction to drugs, food, alcohol, sex, shopping, or work is also a technique for accepting disappointment and smothering our nameless fears.

Depression According to a Harvard Medical School study reported in the *Journal of the American Medical Association* and summarized by Karen Patterson (2003), the current high rate of serious depression is directly related to rapid, sometimes almost numbing, change. In the United States, 16.2 percent of the population—34 million people—will suffer from depression in their lifetime, 6.6 million this year. Depression costs employers $31 billion each year, four times more than the entire year's budget for the National Institutes of Health.

Anxiety Anxiety is a major problem for Americans. More and more of us have become afraid, overwhelmed, trapped, confused, fearful, and rendered cynical by seemingly unpredictable uncertainty and our ineffectual response to it. The *Economist* (1999, p. 28) reported that a poll of 500,000 workers in mid-1999 showed anxiety about jobs to be three times higher than during the recession of 1980–81. Recently, offshore outsourcing has intensified this anxiety. If anxiety is uncontained, the mind retreats into rigidly defensive behavior in an attempt to avoid the anxiety, or it may disintegrate into psychotic fantasy or neurotic acting out (Stacey 1996, p. 129).

Cultural paranoia Paranoia becomes a way of life as we sense attack from unseen agents all around us: germs, viruses, invisible rays in the air (such as microwaves), and even in food full of pesticides, chemicals, and dangerous genetic modifications (Harpur 2002, p. 285). This state of mind of course intensified with events such as the terrorist attacks of September 11 and the spread of mad cow disease.

Perfectionism and procrastination Another negative coping behavior is the trap of perfectionism, which generates procrastination. Trapped by rigid standards and expectations, focusing on past failures, people give little or no credit to their successes. They find anything short of perfect to be unacceptable.

Self-Concealment

Self-concealment seems to be regarded as the most natural state for grown men, and concealment is more natural than candor in our society, according to Sidney Jourard (1971) in *The Transparent Self.* His hypothesis, however, is that we can attain the fullest health and personal development only if we gain the courage to be ourselves with others and if we find goals that have meaning for us. He emphasizes that self-disclosure requires courage—courage to be and to be known! Shall we permit our fellows to know us as we are now, or shall we remain an enigma to be seen as someone we are not? As long as we continue to conceal and box ourselves in from ourselves and others, the chance of moving successfully forward for long-term career satisfaction is slim, if not impossible.

Afraid to Reveal the Truth

Elliot was an attorney and an MBA with outstanding grades from a prestigious school. He miscast himself in the most prestigious law firm and two major consulting firms. He strongly opposed their deal making and their ethics, which were so different from his own. Instead of recognizing the ill fit, he considered himself a failure. However, he did not have the courage to reveal the real truth to others, resulting in problems festering instead of healing.

Shoulds and Oughts

Another major problem in knowing ourselves, in discovering what our internal, instinctive needs really are, is that to compensate for living in an age of unprecedented insecurity, we have learned to base our aspirations on models imposed from without. In addition to who we are fundamentally, we strive to become who we believe we're supposed to be based on these outside models. Many achieve external success—but that kind of success rarely passes for internal fulfillment. In *Earth in the Balance,* Al Gore (1992) reminds us, "The accumulation of material goods is at an all-time high, but so is the number of people who feel an emptiness in their lives." (pp. 221–222).

Frequently, people have problems understanding themselves because they are trying to fit a preconceived mold of what they feel they are expected to be. Carl Jung (1957) says, "It is not the universal or the regular that characterize the individual, but rather the unique" (p. 17). This uniqueness is what we look for in our self-assessment—not how we are standardized like others, but how we are different, and what unique qualities we can bring to the world and the workplace. This is what we're after when adults begin the career enhancement process.

Futile-to-Fight-City-Hall Attitude

In modern society, we are frequently reduced to a statistical number and can feel we have lost our individuality. Many have been taught that the reward of the individual personality is futility and to therefore distrust our instincts. We are expected to go with the masses and not stand as a "majority of one," as Thoreau advises, nor to be self-reliant and trust ourselves as Emerson recommends. "You can't fight city hall," as the saying goes.

When we are so rigidly defined, we don't fit, and we then alter ourselves to produce a fit. This constant alteration leaves us with no inner instinctive direction on which to understand or to build ourselves up. Without this foundation, we accept someone else's agenda and lose or never discover our authentic self. Those individuals who are most successful are the ones with the courage to identify and follow their instincts without thought to fitting a conventional formula.

An important insight from chaos/complexity theory is that one person can make a difference. The "butterfly effect" showed that small, seemingly insignificant, fluctuations can drive and alter a whole system. Similarly, a creative minority in a society can cause a shift to a new order. Those few on the edge pull us gradually toward what will be accepted eventually. The analogy with history is so obvious—the behavior of a small group of people can completely change the behavior of the larger group. Small action can create major change.

AUTHENTIC CHANGE

To understand how adults make needed deep changes, we must examine more thoroughly the factors within the individual that bring new directions and new behavior—those that are so basic that they are really beyond pretense. This is authentic change in the fundamental makeup of the person, not in the external apparel, and when it occurs, the person is genuinely different. This is why I caution that in such a change, we become what we are, not what we think we ought to be. "Authenticity is about living deeply in your own truth. It builds trust because people in your organization, in other businesses, in your community, know where you are really coming from" (Lewin and Regine 2000, p. 308).

Risk Taking

No one can find genuine meaning in life merely by accepting the meaning handed down from others. Many people, for example, are pushed into a career that their parents want them to have or one the parents wished they themselves had had. Personal meaning must be sought out and created, not received, and the process of creating it requires testing and experimentation. A false self will not experiment or risk, but will act as an internal saboteur.

Educated or calculated risk, not impulsivity, is a crucial element in any successful career today, especially a career realignment or change. However, this risk must be tempered with good judgment or it is a liability. If we have a very high risk factor, we should beware. If it's moderate, we are more likely to make sound, practical decisions. If the risk factor is low, then we should begin to develop it, because it will be a necessity in today's world.

Usually, the greater the risk involved in a change, the more information and planning we should exercise in making our decision. Many people are perfectionist victims of "analysis paralysis" and won't give themselves permission to start and learn along the way. They want all the pieces of the puzzle in exactly the right spot before they begin, which is impossible in today's chaotic world.

John Eldredge (2001) writes that all his life he had been asking the world to tell him what to do with himself. This is different from seeking counsel or advice. He said he wanted someone else to tell him who to be, to be free from the responsibility and especially from risk. We are in constant danger of being not actors but reactors in the drama of our own lives.

We must be willing to give ourselves some space and allow ourselves to make mistakes. We can't wait for someone else to tell us what action to take so that we can blame them if it doesn't work. We must create and construct our own dream for ourselves. Each of us has a right to take our life seriously and discover what it is that we are designed by nature to do.

Taking Risks

In his book *Wild at Heart,* John Eldredge (2001) tells about going into a bookstore, idly picking up a book and reading, "Don't ask yourself what the world needs. Ask yourself what makes you come alive, and go do that, because what the world needs is people who have come alive" (p. 200).

Knowing What Is Self-Knowledge

William James (1902) said that most people live in a restricted circle of their potential being, making use of a small portion of their possible consciousness and their soul's resources. Jung (1957), in *The Undiscovered Self,* noted that we frequently confuse "self-knowledge" with knowledge of our ego personality, which is conscious, surface, obvious information only. Anyone who has ego-consciousness at all takes for granted that they know themselves when, in fact, their self-knowledge may be quite minimal. But, as Jung points out, the ego knows only its own contents; it doesn't automatically know the unconscious, which has an abundance of information available to us once we tap into it. We measure only the obvious about ourselves, but frequently we do not factor in the real psychic facts that initially may be hidden. This mostly unaware psychic behavior is like the body with its anatomical structure. Although we live in it and with it, most of the particulars of how it fits together and how it works are totally unknown to us. So what we call "self-knowledge" is therefore often limited, like our knowledge of the body. It is dependent on the social factors of what goes on in the human psyche, and most people remain unaware of it throughout their lives.

For many people, that partially developed surface personality is not even their particular strength and, in reality, may have little real deep connection to them. What they have struggled with and focused on in the past forced them to use their weaknesses, not their strengths. It isn't that they can't perform; it is simply that they have not used their preferred skills or talents, and so have operated minimally on two or three cylinders instead of the possible eight. The result is mediocrity, which, of course, destroys any belief in their abilities.

Recognizing the Shadow Self

According to Carl Jung, in our unconscious, which is immune to conscious criticism and control but has great impact on our behavior, we stand defenseless, open to all kinds of influences and psychic infections. As with all dangers, we can guard against the risk of psychic infection only when we know and understand *what* is attacking us, and how, where, and when the attack might come—in other words, where we are most vulnerable.

This unconscious part of the self Jung calls the "shadow self." Some may interpret this as our "dark side," the negative, unknown parts of ourselves to be ignored and repressed, but according to Jung this is not so. Jung cautions us not to get caught in these negative connotations only. "The shadow is simply the whole unconscious. It's a mythological name for all within me of which I cannot directly know." Jung believed that people instinctively seek to become themselves, but this requires that we understand and accept the seemingly negative parts of ourselves as healthy and useful.

Robert Bly, in *A Little Book on the Human Shadow* (1988), interprets the shadow self as the long bag we drag behind us, heavy with the parts of ourselves that parents and community don't approve of. But to be our authentic self, we need to have insight into this part as well. The necessity for knowing the whole, not just the parts, is a major factor in the new paradigm. The whole is indeed greater than the sum of the parts.

When sunlight hits a body, it illuminates, but also throws a dark shadow. According to Jung, our shadow is the unlit side of our ego. The brighter the light, the darker the shadow. We are urged to acknowledge and accept the visible side of our personality, but each of us has some part of our personality that is hidden from us. The dark and light together unite a whole person, and either alone is not complete. However, our culture teaches us to polarize dark and light, with the conscious and the unconscious in adversarial positions.

A hint to discovering the shadow is to pay close attention to our likes and dislikes and to recognize that perhaps what we see as deviant and intolerable, what we fear and become angry at in others, can be related to the shadow self. We may be particularly sensitive to a quality in someone else that we have been burying in ourselves.

Bly (1988, p. 53) says that when our shadow becomes absorbed, we lose much of our darkness and become light and playful in a new way. In other words, the unabsorbed shadow can darken the air all around a human being. We can sense those who have absorbed or integrated their shadow, those who blend the dark and the light. Bly says they seem to have a "natural authority and authenticity"—a goal worth seeking.

Becoming aware of this unacknowledged, perhaps repressed, side of ourselves can help us to understand what we do to defeat ourselves—the unconscious behaviors that frequently surface under pressure in infantile, childish ways, creating many problems. Being conscious of our shadow self helps us to use it in a planned way. Insight into the shadow self might help us to understand what we do to shoot ourselves in the foot, as well as what we do instinctively and intuitively well. Understanding the duality of our own nature, our potential for good and evil, our strength and weakness, is critical. It puts creative, not rigid, control in our hands.

Self-knowledge takes time. It takes more than a quick fix to free information from the unconscious level and integrate it into conscious self-knowledge. It involves unfreezing our self-concept, our tightly held view of who we are, and letting in new insight and information on the possibilities of what we might have the potential to become. This unfreezing and the deeper opening of the psyche, our unconscious, may come from a variety of new and different experiences, or may come only as a result of dealing with extreme pressure or crisis, through pain, adversity, and even fear. Or it may result from a combination of these two processes. The point is to release and accept your instinctive Meaning Magnet pattern, which comes from your essence, your uniqueness, and is the bedrock that supports and directs you as the complex world shifts around you. It is your consistent "I" that you are surfacing, which will remain constant in spite of chaos, career shock, and collision.

Tapping into Our Talents and Instincts

An artificially developed false self can do fine until a real storm of change hits. This superficial self doesn't have the depth to deal with it. Operating successfully from our true talents and instincts is like having a mysterious Swiss bank account with vast untapped resources that keep expanding. We can actively and successfully tap into it—we can count on this instinctively when it's needed and when we are under pressure! It takes us far beyond the specific knowledge we have consciously acquired. If we don't know what our reserves are, have never consciously tapped and opened them for use, we are setting ourselves up for trouble.

We must look for and accept, indeed, rejoice at our peculiarities. We must embrace our differences and our uniqueness to find our real strengths and to build on them. We need to understand, build on, and manage these strengths and talents instead of focusing on shoring up our weaknesses.

Unfortunately, if our genuine tendencies and instincts are not acknowledged or accepted within our family, school, culture, or workplace, we will assume skills contrary to our own natural ones to fit in, and therefore will never feel fully proficient in them. Consequently, we feel like a stranger to ourselves and in our workplace, never really understanding why. The chronic stress and fallout of being in a career that is contrary—a mismatch to our innate tendencies, our bedrock, our motives, skills, strengths, and values—directly and negatively impacts our self-esteem.

Remembering Our Childhood

In understanding ourselves, we need to recognize that we may have been more our natural selves as children, before we learned the many rules of family and society. We behaved, thought, and felt from a more instinctive creative self. This is not to suggest anarchy or irresponsible, immature behavior. We certainly do not want to act like children; but, rather, we should know that part of ourselves that may have been left behind and now needs attention. Our memories of the past are no random catch-all. We learn from the realization that we hold our particular memories for a reason. In his poem "The Rainbow," William Wordsworth (2000, p. 246) said, "The child is father of the man," and John Milton (2001, p. 346), in *Paradise Regained*, proclaimed, "The childhood shows the man, as morning shows the day."

Success Based on the Authentic Self

Steve graduated from the U.S. Air Force Academy in 1976 and served in the air force as an instructor navigator in the KC-135 air refueling aircraft until 1982. Then he left the military and began a career in the defense industry. Although he put his generalist skills to good use with diverse responsibilities in engineering, finance, marketing, and project management, he always felt a bit like a fish out of water.

Steve decided to cut back on his defense industry job so he could create more time for his passion—writing and teaching about the field known as general semantics. He had served since 1996 as a trustee for the Institute of General Semantics in New Jersey and felt this work was worthy of as much of his time as he could allow. He envisioned working as a part-time consultant so that he could devote more time to the Institute.

Steve boldly ventured out onto a very thin limb. He quit his defense industry job to start an Internet-based business to cater to adult singles. He was convinced this demographic group had a unique set of needs and offered a business opportunity, but he couldn't figure out how to make money with it. In June 2001, he abandoned that idea, sold his house, traded down cars, put his belongings in storage, and decided he would look for a teaching job. Two months of researching and learning about the Texas public school bureaucracy relieved him of that notion.

Embracing his career uncertainty, Steve loaded his car and traveled around the western United States. He was visiting relatives in Washington on September 11, 2001. He immediately headed back home to Dallas. On the way there, he learned that the Institute of General Semantics in New Jersey needed someone to organize sixty years of archives and library materials. Given his interest in and knowledge of the organization, and the fact that he wasn't doing anything else, he volunteered to spend the next three months in New Jersey working in the archives. That led to a part-time job for him with the Institute beginning in 2002, which led to him moving the archives and library to an office in Fort Worth. Steve became the full-time executive director of the organization in January 2004, when the Institute moved to Fort Worth. Steve's career is now in line with his authentic self.

FOUR

Experiencing the Dark Night of Change

*We do not receive wisdom. We must discover it for ourselves after
a journey through the wilderness, which no one else can make for
us, which no one can spare us, for our wisdom is the point of
view from which we come at last to regard the world.*

—MARCEL PROUST

In *The Power of Myth* (1988), which records Joseph Campbell's conversations with Bill Moyers, Campbell talks of the dark night: "One
thing that comes out in myths is that at the bottom of the abyss
comes the voice of salvation. The black moment is the moment when
the real message of transformation is going to come. At the darkest
moment comes the light" (p. 37). He describes the hero's journey as
a life lived in self-discovery. "We find within ourselves the resources
of character to meet our destiny."

Our "dark night" may be a necessity, getting us prepared for our
ultimate success, for it can be the beginning of a step toward continuing change—a requirement in today's environment. Our being
must be lost and then found to be appreciated. Success, not failure, is
built on this. It isn't what happens to us in our lives that is important
so much as how we adapt to and handle it.

The pathfinders for the future, our leaders with confidence in self-renewal, will be those who have gone through the process of change, the dark night of the soul, and no longer find it fearful and alien. They have acquired the capacity and insight to know that success is facing the journey, not the final discovery. If we fear and isolate ourselves from the chaos and change in today's world, we will have nothing to seek. How sad for us, and what a loss for our children and grandchildren, who will need all the positive role models we can provide for dealing successfully with the very real change and complexity of our evolving world.

FACING THE FEAR OF CHANGE

The chaos of change triggers the painful emotional reaction of the process of loss, grief, and fear. For an in-depth exploration of the chaos of change and the dark night of the soul, see Helen Harkness (1997, pp. 133–154). Going through painful experiences can bring us to a keen sense of a truth beyond words and a new path in life. Many people remain unaware of this internal pattern, and frankly they are not in a dark night that initiates change, so they lack the motivation to search for meaning, the strategies to discover it, and the vocabulary to describe it.

Using Change as a Positive Force

The destruction that operates on the edge of chaos *is what makes creative change possible*. To balance our careers on the edge of chaos, we must not hide from or try to eliminate change; rather, we must *use* change as a positive force. The capacity for turning chaos, adversity, and hardship into assets is a skill that can be learned based on our experience.

> Formula for Change
> **C = P > F**
> Change happens only when pain
> is greater than fear.

Crisis as Change Catalyst

We will probably all experience a dark night of the soul. It is important to note that we do have a choice in how to handle it. Realize that this crisis of transformation has opportunity as well as discomfort, like the containment of the caterpillar in the chrysalis before it emerges as a butterfly.

If we can see a crisis as the catalyst for a successful change, we won't waste our time and energy reviling and bewailing. We can put creative energy into digging up what may well have hidden out in our unconscious that is now shooting us in the foot! Successfully navigating the dark night does not mean that life will be a bed of roses after the darkness lifts, but that we will have gained the internal tools to move on with confidence and diminished fear.

The dark night is also a spiritual crisis in that we are searching for meaning and purpose in our life and work. Darkness is a vital part of the journey—life is not a travel package, but a pilgrimage. Hardships are part of it—bad weather, facing down losses—but most people don't talk of their darkness, only their success. Unfortunately, pain precedes the gain, and we are so frequently caught in the pain phase, grieving the loss of the former model of the way things were supposed to be, that we have great difficulty stepping outside of it to map a strategic route to the gain part of the equation.

Finding Meaning in Crisis

According to John Briggs and F. David Peat (1999), going through painful experience "can bring us to a keen sense of truth beyond words and a new path in life" (p. 22). They use Viktor Frankl's life in the Nazi concentration camps to illustrate that "an encounter with the terrible unknown of chaos can bring with it the apparently paradoxical feeling of an intimate, transcending faith or trust in a nurturing cosmos" (p. 164). A sense of solidarity with the entire human race frees us from fear: We know we will survive and thrive.

During his captivity in bestial concentration camps, Viktor Frankl was stripped to a naked existence. He discovered, however, that people who find meaning in a crisis, no matter how terrible, have an easier time getting through. People need an alternative to feeling they have been punished by God or pushed into a random hole of chaos. Frankl (1963, p. 9) echoes Nietzsche: "He who has a why to live can bear with almost any how."

MIDLIFE CRISIS

A classic work relating to meaning is a 1965 paper called "Death and the Midlife Crisis" by Elliott Jacques, a Canadian psychoanalyst. He and later writers observed that somewhere between the ages of thirty-five and fifty, men and women becoming emotionally aware of their mortality may feel that their lives have peaked. At work they may see that advancement and salaries are no longer open-ended. Since there are fewer rungs to climb, they may question whether continued achievement in their area of focus is worth the effort. Competitiveness may recede as they begin to question its overall meaningfulness.

Jacques points out that a person who reaches midlife without having successfully established himself in either marital or occupational life, or if success has been achieved by means of manic activity and denial—with consequent emotional impoverishment—such a person is badly prepared for meeting the demands of middle age and enjoying maturity. James Hillman (1985) speaks of the person as feeling a kind of apathy, described as spiritual dryness—the remoteness of God and the waste of the world. For such a person, handling a successful life and career on the edge of chaos will be impossible.

Alighieri Dante's journey through Hell in *The Divine Comedie* (1994) has become synonymous with the crisis adults frequently experience at midlife. For Dante, it was not the dark world of sin but, as for many today, the world of ignorance, meaninglessness, nothingness, and unknowingness. Like many at midlife, Dante did not understand himself or the purpose of his life, but realized that it required some higher ground, some elevation of perspective, some conceptual picture to perceive and connect all his experiences, some authentic and personal "ahas," which seem to happen as one moves through a dark-night-of-the-soul experience.

Many people today (particularly those of the baby boomer generation) are highly successful on the surface, but lost and searching internally. One of the symptoms of alienation in the modern age is the widespread sense of meaninglessness. Edinger (1992) believes people seek psychotherapy not for a disorder, but because they feel that life has no meaning. Perhaps this has been caused by an unsatisfactory childhood experience or an upheaval occasioned by a major cultural transition such as we are currently experiencing. We have lost our bearings. Our relation to life has become ambiguous. The result is a pervasive feeling of meaninglessness and alienation from life.

Tolstoy's Midlife Crisis

In *The Varieties of Religious Experience* (1902), William James records Tolstoy's dark night and his search for meaning at age fifty, when he was at the height of his literary success:

"Life had been enchanting, it was now flat sober, more than sober, dead. Things were meaningless whose meaning had always been self-evident. The questions 'Why?' and 'What next?' began to beset him more and more frequently. . . . These questions: 'Why?' 'Wherefore?' 'What for?' found no response.' (p. 132).

" 'I felt,' said Tolstoy, 'that something had broken within me on which my life had always rested, and that I had nothing left to hold on to, and that morally my life had stopped. An invincible force impelled me to get rid of my existence, in one way or another' (p. 132).

" 'Behold me then, a man happy and in good health, hiding the rope in order not to hang myself to the rafters of the room where every night I went to sleep alone; behold me no longer going shooting, lest I should yield to the too easy temptation of putting an end to myself with my gun' " (p. 132).

Tolstoy said that he did not know what he wanted, was afraid of life and was driven to leave it. He said that all this took place when he should have been completely happy. He had a good wife, children, large estate, and the respect of all. He said he was neither insane nor ill. " 'And yet I could give no reasonable meaning to any actions of my life. And I was surprised that I had not understood this from the very beginning' " (p. 133).

He thought of suicide almost constantly (p. 134), but gradually, after about two years, he began to move out of his dark night. He saw his problems in life as being those of the upper, intellectual, artistic classes—the life he had always led. " 'The cerebral life, the life of conventionality, artificiality and personal ambition. He had been living wrong and must change' " (p. 158). He embraced the life of the peasant and felt happy.

LETTING GO AND TAKING HOLD

By letting go of consensual structures and conventional wisdom, a creative self-organization becomes possible. If we are to solve the major problems of chaos and uncertainty, we must gain a new consciousness of the world into which we are moving. Quite simply, a major event such as a negative career problem involves two different processes: letting go and taking hold. The letting go is the turning loose and falling apart of the old; and the renewal is the taking hold of the new. These processes are connected by a transition time, a bridge, a time of chaos—by a dark night of the soul. On the edge of chaos, we relinquish parts of the past and begin to take hold of the future at the same time.

This is a crucial period of both vulnerability and potential. The breaking apart and falling away of the old career system, the former structure, beliefs, and self-concept as we have known it, is the first step. The chaos, disorder, and uncertainty that accompany this breakdown are necessary parts of the process.

The second step of the change process is a rebuilding, a renewal, or discovery of a career identity and focus. A successful career on the edge of chaos today cannot be based merely on the identification of what the current marketplace will buy. To be successful and significant there must be a shift in identity to that of our authentic self and the discovery of unused parts of ourselves and of our Meaning Magnets. These must then be tied to the needs of the outer world for which they can feel a response or connection.

It is important to examine and understand how internal human change occurs—what factors are involved deeply within the individual, and which polarize new directions and new behavior. What are the basic factors beyond a person's power of dissimulation or pretense, so that when change occurs, the person will be different, moved, shifted inside, changed, in order to go successfully into the new career field?

Managing our careers in today's uncertainty is a nonlinear process that proceeds not in clear-cut, predictable steps, but in spurts, pauses, and leaps. Individuals do not complete the internal process of realigning their careers on a timeline. The process takes a right- *and* left-brain approach, connecting and using the logical and rational, as well as the intuitive and creative, with gut-level decisions.

This career process can be multifaceted, fluid, dynamic, astounding, and only partly controllable. Because of this, and because many of us in real chaos have spent so much energy and effort controlling and keeping ourselves tightly wrapped in order to be who we think we are, or ought to be, or might become, that it is very difficult to let go. We have accumulated this false self so carefully—following a rigid formula—that turning loose even momentarily seems like doom.

When faced with change that seems out of our control, we panic. Keeping the false self together has allowed no awareness of the authentic self, no core instincts of being to guide us under pressure. With no consistent "I," we are strangers to ourselves. When we do not fit our work—or for whatever reason our work fails to reinforce, revitalize, or renew us—we join the lonely crowd, isolated but not autonomous.

DROPPING THE MASK

According to Carl Jung (1957), when we must wear a mask, we assume a persona. This is our public personality, a facade presented to satisfy the demands of an external world or situation, but which does not represent the inner personality of our authentic self. In other words, when we must wear a mask to fit our career, we are playing a role. In Chapter 3, we referred to this persona as our false self.

When we avoid using our authentic self to understand our strengths and needs, we reject our human imperfections, strive for rigid perfectionism, and focus constantly on shoring up our weaknesses. This loss of authentic self and assumption of a false self sets us up for personal and career problems. Many people talk about the real fear involved in "discovering who they really are."

The more successful we are at work while being this false self, and the more reinforcement we get for it, the more it negatively impacts our self-esteem. If there is little or no opportunity to be authentic and real, we can't develop and grow our strengths naturally, in a way that defines and refines our strengths. We don't know who we are, what we can do, or where we belong. Searching for the authentic self can be frightening and lonely, and thus we cling to the false self because it is what we know. To begin to release this false self can be frightening, even as we search for real self-identity. With its uncertain outcome, this time of searching contributes to our dark night of the soul.

When, for external or internal reasons, we must face the necessity of dropping the mask, we feel exposed and may experience fear. People in this situation describe the fear as akin to facing a kind of death of self, even if the former self has ceased to operate satisfactorily. There is a perhaps unconscious fear that if we let go of the former identity or self-concept, especially before there is a clearly defined one to replace it, we will become nothing, a nobody, and may cease to exist.

Yet, we must drop the mask and release the false self to discover and create the authentic self. We can't create or gain a new career identity while still holding tightly to the former one. There doesn't seem to be room in our psyche for these two identities. It is painful to release the familiar (even though it is negative), to search for the unknown and the unfamiliar, which is populated by other realities, fears, and anxieties that we cannot even name. Plato, in the Seventh Book of his *Republic* (1968), compares such unenlightened men, those unwilling to face the unfamiliar, to prisoners in a dark cave, a den.

All initiations require a separation phase: being pulled gently or violently from the familiar—from family, friends, behavioral habits, and accustomed ways of thinking or feeling. We can leave home but carry all our teaching with us, so physical leaving may not be enough. We must discover, develop, and struggle with our own strengths and shortcomings. We have absorbed thoughts, feelings, and actions from others, and these inner patterns lie unexamined in us. When we begin to question their truth and value, as Linda Sussman (1995) says, this is the beginning of learning.

THE BEST PART OF THE JOURNEY

We can relate to Dante, Tolstoy, and others because they genuinely admit to their human problems and failures and have ceased to pretend to superficial values. Like many of us on the journey to emotional maturity, such seekers become aware that they have reached an impasse, a psychological place that can no longer be ignored if they are to continue growing. Our journey at this time can be our very best. If handled successfully, we can enjoy a strong sense of freedom, control, and confidence.

Here are four power points that guide this change process:

1. Maintaining tight, rigid control, "living life's lie" creates a personal prison; turning loose and facing your worst fears and moving through them creates personal power and the freedom to become your authentic self.

2. Beware the tyranny of authority and the conventional wisdom that goes against your intuition. Trust your instincts; they become more powerful with use! If you never use them (and perhaps risk some failure) they will never become keen and well developed—the important resource that they can be.

3. Ask for and accept help when needed. Needing help signals not a pathetic victim but an authentic person who can connect in a genuine manner with others. When you resolve to move forward and use your pain and chaos and the help you received to heal others, you become strong. Build relationships and be there for others when they need you.

4. Real security is internal, not external. Your strengths, talents, skills, knowledge, insight, and instinct for survival are not in another person, a particular situation, or an object, but in the genuine connection with the authentic self and others.

The first part of our life happens to us, and mostly we have played it by all the traditional and conventional rules. But now with our increased maturity, experience, independence, and wisdom gained from our time of dark night, we can feel free to choose and customize. This is liberating, but somewhat unnerving at the same time. Rick Warren, in *The Purpose Driven Life* (2002), assures us that "your most effective ministry will come out of your deepest hurts" (p. 275).

The Author's Personal Journey Through the Dark Night

After seventeen years of marriage, my husband and I were building our dream home. Unfortunately, however, the marriage was falling apart, held together, as I saw it, only through my sheer drive to make it work. It was out of control, and I was grimly hanging on because that's what I had been trained to do by the culture of my era. "Never walk away from something you started—never give up," was the message and, combined with the fear of having failure on my life's record, my years of emotional and financial investment, and my own insecurity about the future, turning loose, I must admit, didn't seem an option.

Maintaining the community image of the physician's wife, I was living opposed to my authentic self and had developed outward control and poise—a mask, a wall. My attitude was that I had to handle these problems myself. I could never reveal the real situation or be indebted to anyone. I ferociously expected myself to handle all things perfectly, remain proud, and never let down my emotional defenses. I made absolutely certain that I was indebted to no one. No one did more for me than I did for them. This created a closed system, where I felt everything was totally my burden. I had gotten myself into the problem, and it was my responsibility to get out of it on my own.

Things became intolerable and, telling no one but my husband, I did find courage to file for a divorce. One week later, between Christmas and New Year's, three months after the house was completed, the house caught fire from the aluminum wiring, a seemingly common architectural disaster in the 1970s.

That fire seemed to be the catalyst in my chaotic life. I stood out in front on the hill, watching the flames leap from the roof. I thought of all my books, first editions, and hundreds of contemporary books, signed and carefully collected—no chance to get all those out—and too late for family pictures. But the children were safe with me, and even the cats and Sam, the Basset hound, hovered nearby.

Then somehow, strangely, I began to feel strongly light and free. I didn't feel fearful or frightened. I thought, I've done all I can. I can turn loose and move on. It's over. In such an apparent disaster, I didn't have to be in control of it all! By turning loose of tight control, I seemed to gain a sense of direction and real control.

Almost like a miracle, the fire was put out, leaving much smoke and water damage, but burning only one room completely. Yet I instinctively did not trust that it was completely out. Maybe my mother's earlier admonitions (her family's home burned when she was young) about fires smoldering and flaring up again, even days later, was the source of this instinct. So I trailed after the fire chief and asked him if he was certain the fire was out. I probably repeated this question more than he liked, but for whatever reason, he finally drew himself up to his 6'4", 240 lbs. of manhood, and looking down on me, impatiently said, "The fire is absolutely out! I have told you the fire is out! I know my job. I have been in this business for thirty years. How long have you been fighting fires?" I will never forget standing ankle deep in burned Christmas decorations, in the rain, muck, and smoke, and feeling properly chastised, humbled, like a child—thinking to myself, "Why can't you simply accept authority?"

Nevertheless, I spent the night with my children at the next-door neighbor's house. At 4:00 a.m. I awoke abruptly to the sound and sight of crackling flames, fire truck sirens, and the stench of smoke. My home burned to the ground.

That morning after the fire and throughout the day in freezing drizzle, at least fifty neighbors, friends, and even strangers who were driving by took over a great task. I was in a daze. My earlier euphoria of freedom had passed, and my sense of direction and leadership had fizzled. I felt lost, homeless, numb. My friends and neighbors organized, carried out, picked up, rented storage; took care of the dog, the cats; rented an apartment close by and moved me, the children, and the pets. Dozens sloshed around in rain, sleet, and mud all day until late evening. It was truly remarkable.

For months after I completed the rebuilding, these friends, neighbors, and strangers returned salvaged pictures, pieces of furniture, and mementos they had cleaned, repaired, and restored. What an outpouring of help and support! It was unbelievable. There was no way I could ever repay their timely kindness, attention, and labor. All I could do was humbly and gratefully thank them, resolve to get my life back together, and position myself to eventually pass the same help on to others who found themselves in similar troubling chaos. This has been the strongest motivation for much I have done since then.

Career success today requires that we drop the protective armor of the self-defeating false self, a remnant of the career paradigm. Replacing that armor with the skills required in the new edge-of-chaos career paradigm requires knowing the authentic, real self. The assessment on the following pages will help you determine where you are in the process.

SELF-INVENTORY OF YOUR CAREER PARADIGM

Directions: *Place a check mark to the left of traits that describe you. Total the number of checks for each column to provide a self-inventory of whether your career model is in the past or current. Check the self-defeating traits you may want to begin to change.*

Old Career Paradigm	Edge-of-Chaos Career Paradigm
☐ Money matters	☐ Meaning matters
☐ Bottom line: here and now only	☐ Foresight, future orientation
☐ Powerless and apathy	☐ Self-reliance and vitality
☐ Fear self-promotion: don't know or ask for what you want	☐ Know what you want, ask for it efficiently, and know you deserve it
☐ Fear of failure or fear of success	☐ Courage, positive resilience
☐ Play it safe, avoid risks	☐ Calculated, educated risk taking
☐ See self as victim, hopelessly trapped	☐ Learn from pain and failure and move on
☐ Controlled by others	☐ Self-directed
☐ Overreliance on others, conventional wisdom, tyranny of authority	☐ Aware of and trust self and instincts, think outside the box—sharp crap detector
☐ Passive, deferring, directionless	☐ Choose battles—say "NO" without guilt
☐ Perfectionism: "everything is important and MUST be done exactly right"	☐ Prioritize problems: determine whether they are serious offenses or merely misdemeanors
☐ Procrastination, indecision, waiting	☐ Design plan and take action
☐ Need high structure and organization	☐ Live with ambiguity and uncertainty
☐ Rigid, analytical—"either/or" dualistic thinking	☐ Creativity, flexibility, intuitive "both/and" approach

Old Career Paradigm	Edge-of-Chaos Career Paradigm
☐ Closed system: satisfied with present knowledge, no questions or concerns	☐ Curiosity, begin, learn, question: practice art of inquiry
☐ Judgmental, controlling, isolated	☐ Contacting, connecting, communicating
☐ Aloof, hostile, defensive, suspicious	☐ Open, authentic, real, optimistic
☐ Cynicism, despair	☐ Upbeat skepticism
☐ Follow conventional path—carefully stay in the mainstream at all costs	☐ Become a boundary breaker, a "tempered radical," comfortable at the edges
☐ Stay with the herd	☐ Realize that the majority is often wrong
☐ Shore up weaknesses	☐ Build on strengths and talents
☐ Career on automatic pilot—takes care of itself	☐ Create a career contingency plan
☐ Sugarcoat, solve problems after they occur	☐ Scout problems before they occur
☐ Mask to maintain conforming image	☐ Authenticity—flexibility to divulge individuality
☐ Freedom from responsibility	☐ Freedom with responsibility
☐ Problems and fault caused by others	☐ Sense of personal powers
☐ Information—answers, facts, certainty of experience	☐ Insight—ask questions, learn to accept uncertainty
☐ Bound by human limitations.	☐ Belief in possibility of accomplishments beyond the ordinary
Total Checks for Former Career Model	**Total Checks for Current Career Model**

PART II

REDESIGNING
OUR CAREERS

Even today, remarkably few Americans are prepared to select jobs for themselves. When you ask, "Do you know what you are good at? Do you know your limitations?" they look at you with a blank stare. Or they often respond in terms of subject knowledge, which is the wrong answer.

—PETER DRUCKER

Career success requires living, working, thinking, and creating on the edge of chaos, between rigid structures and frozen rules on one side and disorder on the other. How do we accomplish this? Part I presented the following guidelines:

1. Discover and understand your unique Meaning Magnets.

2. Cultivate the Type CC (change catalyst) personality, replacing the Type A and Type B personalities of the past.

3. Distinguish your authentic self from your false self, and use your authentic self as the basis on which to build your life and career on the edge of chaos.

4. Understand that career success is a highly creative process. Creativity lies at the edge of disintegration, and the creative process in human systems is inevitably messy—this may initiate a journey through the dark night, involving differences, conflict, fantasy, and the emotions of fear, anger, envy, and depression.

In Part II, we will look at a four-step career design process that will use these concepts to allow us to redesign and take creative charge of our careers. Each of these steps is presented in Chapters 5 through 8: Looking Inward, Looking Outward, Looking Forward, and Taking Action. In Chapter 9, Looking Beyond, we will look at chaos and change in organizations.

FIVE

Looking Inward

Fifteen or twenty years ago people were asking, "How can we prepare ourselves for our next promotion?" Now they ask, "What do I need to learn so that I can decide where to go next?"

—PETER DRUCKER

Our career design process is intended to help you understand and honor your uniqueness. Our perspective is to have you stand back from yourself and pick out the unique patterns that make you you. It is imperative that you become an expert at discovering, describing, applying, practicing, and refining your strengths. The first step of the career design process is looking inward for answers to *Who am I?* and *What can I do?*

THE PLACE FOR
THE CAREER ASSESSMENT TOOL

There are well-researched, reliable, formal career assessment tools that can help identify temperament tendencies, options, and ideas (see, for example, http://career-design.com/self_ profile.html). These tools can tie into and suggest a variety of specific career fits, but they do not give final answers. For a serious career issue, it is necessary to go beyond such assessments. People in severe career crisis often hope for a quick fix. Many would like to take a test that would tell them what to do for the rest of their life. They see such tests as silver bullets: magically, quickly, and accurately providing the total solution to their career predicament. But tests are like materials used to build a house—they must be assembled as part of a coherent plan. Tests taken or given in a vacuum may never be fully interpreted or completely understood.

That being said, valid assessments can be a first step in providing the following:

- A system and a vocabulary for understanding yourself and the career matches that surface from the answers you provided

- Initial direction and insight—but you first must understand what specifically is being assessed

- Confirmation that you may be in the right career, but in the wrong work environment

- General direction—don't expect absolute answers and don't necessarily buy into the careers given

It is important to have a qualified professional interpret test results, since people may read results, make premature conclusions, and never think deeply about themselves.

INSIGHTS INTO OUR MEANING MAGNETS

As we discussed in Chapter 2, each of us has deep roots, basic patterns or essences as unique as our fingerprints, which we call our Meaning Magnets. These deeply embedded, recurring, interwoven patterns of behavior are at the core of who we are. They reflect our basic needs and interests, our style, temperament, personality, skills, and motives. The design is already within us; our challenge is to uncover the patterns and then determine how and where to build our future using these essences.

A Meaning Magnet is a consistent, unique, and major payoff for you. You experience a payoff anytime you do something that gives you great satisfaction and a sense of achievement. Meaning Magnets are unique to the individual, but could include, for example, the need for constant challenge, being an expert, managing, creating something new, thinking of new ideas, starting things up, serving others, maintaining a simple and balanced lifestyle, experiencing excitement, meeting challenges, gaining recognition, solving unique problems, having an influence, being on a constant learning curve, overcoming obstacles, leading others, and being independent.

A Meaning Magnet for the Author

I am a grower—of people, ideas, trees, and plants. As a teacher and a naturalist, I am delighted when a client moves forward or when a plant puts out new leaves or branches. It isn't necessary for the plant to be exotic or unusual, but merely for it to grow in its natural way and place.

For an assessment tool or another person to simply tell us our Meaning Magnet pattern is not fully effective. We must consciously see and name the patterns of behavior created by our attractions so we can systematically, not randomly, keep the patterns at center stage in our next career move. We need to see how the patterns connect with the reality of our own life. Meaning Magnets are based on our authentic self, and finding our Meaning Magnets gives us clues to discovering the core of our being. To be in creative control of our career, we must discover and name the unique patterns that identify us.

To begin to discover your Meaning Magnets, complete Activity 1, below.

ACTIVITY 1: Finding Clues to Your Meaning Magnets

Obtain a small notebook to carry in your purse or pocket for one month.

- *Each time you identify a factor deeply and unquestionably essential in your personal and professional life, write it down.*

- *Jot down any "ahas!" that occur to you.*

- *Think about your daydreams and aspirations and record those you can remember.*

- *Think about their relationship to each other and to your current career and past careers. Are there elements that tie daydreams and aspirations together?*

Steve's Meaning Magnets

When Steve, the former air force instructor navigator who wanted to work in the field of semantics, began looking at his Meaning Magnets, he discovered he wanted to

- Leave his mark on the people and organizations he became involved with

- Improve things, to make people/things work or operate better, and pass on these improvements or lessons learned to others

- Make a difference

- March to his own drummer

IDENTIFYING PAST ACCOMPLISHMENTS

Everyone has achievements that are personally important to them. These are not necessarily accomplishments people would talk about in a formal interview setting, but they involve times when people feel like they are riding the waves of fulfillment—when everything falls into the right place for them.

Recalling and analyzing what you consider your past accomplishments can be enlightening. Some people may work through this exercise quickly, giving it only surface attention and not much thought. For others this assignment can be a very real challenge at first. Some people have been or are currently in therapy and are recalling painful, embarrassing, or self-defeating incidents. Others are in negative work environments and haven't thought about *anything* positive for quite a while. And there are a few who have just never thought about a positive accomplishment in their adult lives, but can readily verbalize many negative incidents.

It is not unusual for people who may be very successful financially to never mention any accomplishment related to their current job or career field. Also, the particular span of years one remembers as being filled with the most accomplishments can be significant; some years may yield few if any accomplishments. Many people recall experiences from their younger years before their formal career began.

David Viscott (1976, p. 27) reminds us that the defenses that block unpleasant memories also block pleasurable ones. This inability to remember what is positive robs us of energy and joy and prevents us from forming an optimistic attitude. James Masterson (1988, p. 24) says that if we use our own unique style in an accomplishment, it will integrate and reinforce our self-image and self-esteem—this is what we are taking the time and process to determine. The goal is to get to the authentic self in a positive way.

You may be used to judging an accomplishment to be significant only if it is considered so by the external world. You must begin to identify an accomplishment as something with importance and value to *yourself.*

Learning to verbalize your talents, strengths, and skills will help you to acquire a vocabulary for consciously naming them as well as the ability to identify them. This is especially important in today's workplace. Activity 2 is designed to help you remember and identify these talents.

ACTIVITY 2: Positive Accomplishments of Your Life

Recall and list at least three *accomplishments from each stage of your life that meet these criteria: (1) you did it well, (2) you enjoyed doing it, and (3) you felt proud of it.*

Childhood Years

Ages 13–17

Ages 18–21

Ages 22–24

Ages 25–29

Ages 30–34

Ages 35–39

Ages 40–44

Ages 45–49

Age 50 and above

Allow some time to reflect, mull, and muse. Then select five accomplishments from your list—from any age or setting that you feel is most important to you. Using index cards, record each of these accomplishments on one card.

On each of the cards, list the talents, strengths, and skills required for the particular accomplishment you have listed.

Sort through the cards to select and prioritize what you listed as the skills and talents exhibited in each accomplishment.

Steve's Accomplishments

The final accomplishment I related concerned a one-act play I wrote for a creative writing class I took at the Air Force Academy. The play, "The Unveiling of Ourselves," was written as a morality play to express concerns I had at the time regarding the failure of people to assert their independence and individuality while falling victim to either the influence of peer pressures or the seduction of the ways of the world. Reflecting back on that theme years later, I'm amazed that, in a sense, my entire adult life has been spent grappling with the same issues that the protagonist faced in trying to unveil his own true self. The play won an award for the best one-act play and was published in the annual collection of creative writing produced by the Department of English and Fine Arts.

Here are some of the talents, skills, and abilities I learned I have:

- Creativity and intelligence
- A sense of responsibility to perform, to accomplish, and to improve on the activities I participate in
- Ability to function within a team or organizational environment, while also maintaining an obvious individuality and nonconforming attitude

I thought about how easy it has been for me to overlook and underappreciate my own talents and skills and about how I tend to erroneously assume that what comes easy to me does so for everybody else.

IDENTIFYING OUR SUCCESS CRITERIA

Peter Drucker, in responding to Bill Moyers' (1989) asking what advice he would give young people who are trying to get ready for the twenty-first century, replied that *knowing your strengths, what you are good at, is most important.* "Very few people know that. All of us know what we're not good at. But the reason why so few of us know what we're good at is that it comes so easy. You sweat over what's hard to do. So knowing what you're good at is the first thing" (p. 410). Having intimate knowledge of talents that we can consciously pursue with purpose, as well as identifying the possible environments needing these talents, establishes a source of certainty in our world.

Success criteria are the *specific* personal and professional imperatives we must have to feel successful. They are tied together by our Meaning Magnets—the patterns we are drawn to automatically. Our success criteria are our top priorities in our work and personal lives. We can think of them as "glass balls" because they demand attention and care and should not be ignored or dropped and broken. We must also recognize the "rubber balls," the cluster of less important issues that clutter up life but that can be dropped without creating any problem. After you have read through Steve's success criteria, begin the process suggested in Activity 3.

Steve's Success Criteria

For my success criteria—my glass balls—I want and need the following:

- To interact with knowledgeable, competent people
- To be free from financial worries on a modest scale: not motivated to make money, just not having to worry about making money
- Positive recognition
- Flexibility to organize, plan, communicate, synthesize, and so on, according to my own priorities

---

ACTIVITY 3: Your Success Criteria

- *Make a chart of your success criteria, using Joel's chart (see Figure 1, on page 70) as a template if you wish.*

- *List your previous, current, and possible future careers.*

- *List your success criteria.*

- *Assign a numerical value to how well these criteria are satisfied in each job.*

Joel Examines His Career Success

I was born in New York, and ever since I can remember, I was told by my father that making money should be my first priority. I originally wanted to major in oceanography, but my father said, "No, business only!" even though I was paying my own tuition. I enjoyed many leadership opportunities in college and excelled early on as a dorm proctor. At the end of my senior year, a major advertising agency was actively recruiting me, and, in retrospect, this would have been a better career fit for me. But, with my father's encouragement, I went into business marketing and later into investment banking.

I fell headlong into the career myth that hard work, perseverance, and company loyalty would secure my place within my firm and secure my personal wealth. Nothing could have been farther from the truth. After a company bankruptcy and relocation, I found myself with no job and on the brink of serious depression caused by my naïve sense of loyalty and a driven internal need for approval. When I finally lifted my head out of the sand, I realized with a deep disappointment that I had spent twenty-one years pursuing a career path that didn't energize or excite me.

When I began to list my success criteria, I was shocked to realize that the financial and some knowledge criteria were the only ones being met in my previous career.

Thoughtfully determine and list the specific personal and professional imperatives you must have to feel successful. Rate criteria 1 to 10 (10 being the highest). List former jobs or those being considered. →	INVESTMENT BANKING				
My Success Criteria					
Must have financial support of myself and family, ability to pay for college and retirement	8				
Company's values must reflect those of my religious faith and ethics	2				
Some routine is OK, but must be able to multitask	2				
Leaders' goals and company atmosphere must be in line with my own thinking	2				
Must be involved in decision process for job and future	2				
Must be able to learn about company (develop into a specialty)—growing, cutting-edge ideas	4				
Must have flexibility to set own schedule	2				
Must work with creative types or create something to sell	2				
Must feel pride in product or position that fills an important need	2				
Option Totals	26				

Figure 1—Joel's Success Criteria

DETERMINING A CAREER IDENTITY BASED ON THE AUTHENTIC SELF

Determining a new career identity based on the authentic self is a challenge and can be a most complex process and therefore not instant or automatic. It does provide clients exploring career enhancement the opportunity to get all of life's pattern pieces brought to the surface and evaluated. We seek nothing less than genuine self-awareness and authenticity. This is our bedrock, our fundamental foundation, which may shift under pressure but not crack.

Our Meaning Magnet patterns are the roots that go deep and thrive and will not dramatically shift even as the work changes. They will be just as true in the future as in the present, though we will certainly continue to grow, adapt, expand, and add to them. When we know what we are all about, we can adjust our careers in the future while maintaining the stability of our basic foundation. Knowing one's identity and instinctive pattern of behavior based on our Meaning Magnets is the one real security in the chaotic, upside-down work world. Genuine career and self-knowledge and the vision and will to act on it (as discussed in Chapter 6) are the keys to thriving and maintaining creative control over careers on the edge of chaos.

A Testimony of Search for the Authentic Self— Brenda's Story

What I have learned about my authentic self is that relationships are everything! This is and has always been my talent and my Meaning Magnet. Being able to build, nurture, and keep long-term relationships does not come easily to everyone.

When I first embarked on my career, relationships were key to my landing my first job out of college. I didn't realize it at the time, but looking back, it is so obvious. The year was 1988 and I was a senior marketing student at the University of Wyoming.

Unfortunately, very few firms were recruiting on campus. Wyoming does not have a strong commercial base, and the economy was keeping companies from other states from recruiting there.

At the time, I was part of the Dean's Advisory Council. This was a group of student leaders and professors, including the dean of the business school. We met to address timely issues, concerns, and ideas for the business college. Of course, the hottest topic was How are we going to get hired? One of our professors at the time, an entrepreneurial man, came up with the idea to hold a job fair in Dallas. He had the contacts there and helped us get the commitment of nine Dallas-based firms. Forty students from Wyoming attended the job fair. That is where I interviewed and was offered a position with Texas Instruments.

The point is that I wouldn't have had this opportunity without the relationships of the Dean's Advisory Council, and we wouldn't have had the participation without our professor's relationships that brought about the firms' commitments.

Since that time fifteen years ago, I have been building relationships in the Dallas area. People always comment that I am good at keeping in touch. I offer to help with a problem, or make an introduction, or provide a good referral. It is just something I do. For example, I was interested in learning more about the Suzuki method of learning piano and violin. I got a recommendation from the parents' network for a certain teacher. I attended the parent training classes and later decided that my son wasn't ready for this type of commitment. However, I have since referred two friends who have now been with this teacher for three or four years.

I still didn't realize how valuable my relationships were until very recently. After ten years with the corporate scene, I left to try to find a more satisfying career fit. My first move was to a small company in a business development role. Business development was great, but I didn't like passing off my clients to the "service" department, who then often didn't follow though.

Recently I became a loan officer. This is a great role for me for many reasons. I generate all my own business, but I also serve my clients. I have a need for both independence and belonging, which can be a potential conflict. What I have found is that the "belonging" can be with your "network" as opposed to your "employer." As I was discovering this, I also realized that I couldn't afford to look at my business as transactional. If I did, I would be starting over every month. I started to view myself as a life-long value-added advisor to my clients. I told them what I meant by this. In parallel, I joined a professional, formal networking group that is committed to a "give first" philosophy.

When asked by my boss and colleagues at the mortgage company how I was getting my business, I explained that I am genuinely interested in others. So—I ask them about their businesses, their jobs, their families, their homes, and so on. Most people will then ask me about myself. Once you start relating with others, you find common ground and often the topic of home financing comes up. This seems so obvious and straightforward, but, amazingly, others figure that I tell everyone I'm a loan officer. Well, only once have I established a valid relationship or reason to mention this fact.

I also subscribe to a formal referral-based business design. I keep in touch on a regular basis with my clients and my sphere of influence. I always ask if there is anything I can do for them. It may not be related to home financing; it may be they need a referral to a trade or a service. They may be looking for a job, or they may need some feedback about something. They decide on the value that I bring. And when they have a need for home financing or when they get into conversations where home financing comes up, they think of me first. They become comfortable referring me.

My relationships are my fortune. This is a long-term approach. You don't know who will become your biggest advocate—you have to keep reaching out and adding value away from your "sale."

SIX

Looking Outward

*Everything I thought I knew about leadership is wrong. Everything
had changed—technology, customers, the environment around
customers, the market. The people in the organization and what
they wanted from their work had changed.*

**—MORT MEYERSON TO ROSS PEROT, after being
out of the business for five years and then
returning to Perot Systems**

In the previous chapter we took the first step of learning to live and
work on the edge of chaos: looking inward to gain insight and a connection with our authentic self. Now it is time to look outward—to
match our authentic self with the opportunities and realities of the
external world.

ACTIVATING THE CAREER DESIGN PROCESS

Through looking inward, we can know ourselves and determine
what has meaning and purpose, but this must be connected to the
external world in an effective way. The looking outward stage begins
an active part of our career design process. This is a stage of

researching and discovering a match for our Meaning Magnets and our success criteria. The conscious integration of the internal with external realities is essential, but it is not necessarily a linear, step-by-step process. For many of us, however, just visualizing ourselves moving forward in an active, positive, believable way in a career lights the fire in our search and acts as a strong motivation to take the necessary action.

Knowing we have career options is a stimulus and strong driver to keep us moving in what can be a challenging time. Looking outward means researching and skill building—not searching for a job, but seeking information and insight on a career match.

A Nonlinear Career Design

Deciding where to go next in your career today is not a simple task. Building a successful career on the edge of chaos is quite contrary to the "one life equals one career" ideal, so much rethinking is required. In reality, careers no longer move in the linear, discrete, and logical steps of the organizational management ladder or steady-state professional specialist, such as a lawyer, a physician, or a teacher. Careers shift in different directions, at times rapidly and then in agonizing slowness. Genuine internal insight may not produce overt change for a time. Career change can be a major shift in direction but with related connections, as with two of my physician clients—one is becoming a biotechnology entrepreneur, and the other is taking the initial steps to create a holistic wellness center.

Zigzagging

In his essay "Self Reliance," Ralph Waldo Emerson (1909, p. 71) said, "The voyage of the best ship is a zigzag line of a hundred tacks. See the line from a sufficient distance, and it straightens itself to the average tendency."

Some Cautionary Notes

Do your own smart zigzagging by considering these cautionary notes.

On taking a bridge job People in career transition come from all levels—highly educated professionals in law, medicine, and technology and business entrepreneurs; homemakers now trying to translate volunteer leadership talent into a paying job; non-English-speaking garment industry workers; and young unwed mothers with limited education and no formal work experience. The career design process will vary with the needs of each client.

If you must first address the necessity for immediate income, you will need to get a bridge job—one in which you can be productive and have an income. It is impossible to think creatively about the future if you cannot pay the rent. A bridge job can provide relief from intense financial pressure, so you can focus on the process of researching and discovering career options and, later on, clarifying a vision of the future career and the action steps to get there. Even if you are not having financial problems, you may take a bridge job because you need to begin a trial run to explore and understand a particular working situation. In any case, be careful not to confuse this bridge job with the final career focus!

On taking your time Feeling a need for a career identity and wanting to quickly move from uncertainty, you may want to jump immediately into a new career after getting only superficial information on possible matching careers. You may be tempted to skip the research and future thinking, which determine a genuine match of careers to your authentic self. It is critical to realize that all career fields are in climactic change and flux. What a career has been or where it has been headed, even in the recent past, could be dramatically different from what it is today. New, previously unheard-of fields may now become possible matching opportunities. Careful research on the current reality is essential.

On going back to school Many will want to immediately run back to the academic world to solve career issues. This decision can easily be made too quickly. Often people have returned to academia and accumulated impressive degrees but have no real idea how to use them. Unfortunately, when they determine what it is they really need to do based on the authentic self, they often find that a very different degree would have been an advantage.

If you do decide to return to school, make sure you have a definite plan. For example, Sandy has a Ph.D. in microbiology and was working in a drug-testing lab, though originally she had wanted to go to medical school. While working in the lab, because she enjoyed teaching, she had also taught anatomy at the community college. Thorough research and self-knowledge led her to combine health care and teaching: She is now in nursing school with a plan to become a nurse educator. This decision was made carefully, not hurriedly.

When you are there, be sure not to hide behind the academic walls. Spend 25 percent of your energy and focus in making contacts for employment when you graduate.

PRACTICING THE ART OF INQUIRY

Practicing the art of inquiry—asking meaningful questions—is a skill related to dealing with contradiction and uncertainty in an era of information overload. We need to ask questions without a rigid emphasis on one right answer and to be wary of seeking quick, simple answers to complex issues. If we move into small, comforting, familiar boxes that close out the rest of the world, we will fail to see new insights and messages for our future.

Knowing how to ask the right questions in today's world is absolutely critical. Many of us, especially women and those of the Silent Generation, were taught to listen carefully, with the hope that the answer to our questions would somehow surface. If a question occurs to you, trust that it's worth asking! Einstein told us, "Learn from yesterday, live for today, hope for tomorrow. The important thing is to not stop questioning" (Arlington Institute 2004, p. 13).

The Legend of Percival

Percival was reared in a deep forest and carefully taught by his mother to be a passive onlooker and never ask questions, thereby avoiding all trouble. He accidentally wandered into the Castle of the Grail, which was under a demon's spell that could be broken only by an innocent fool asking a simple question. Though Percival saw wondrous things, including the Grail itself, and was curious, he obeyed his former teachings and asked no questions. He missed the opportunity to break the spell and gain fame, and he spent the rest of his life searching.

Asking the "Grail questions," in Activity 4—those that give meaning, sound information, and insight to understanding the next career focus—is an important exercise. Know the key questions about a career field for which you are curious to discover answers.

ACTIVITY 4: Asking the Grail Questions

- *Decide who would be the best people to talk with, both for information and for advice relating to the career fields that really interest you.*

- *Research the library and the Internet to obtain solid background information for your questions.*

- *Ask strong, thoughtful, meaningful Grail questions, which transmit meaning and inspire change by giving the recipients the freedom to choose and create as they reply.*

RESOURCES FOR CAREER INFORMATION

Consider the following potential resources in your community.

- Churches and nonprofit community groups can provide help, such as job search and networking groups.

- Professional meetings and conventions for specific career fields are excellent places for gathering information and insight into how you relate to others in a particular field. Examining publications from professional organizations and special interest groups is also helpful.

- Check the newspaper for community events, speeches, and presentations that may be of interest to you.

- Colleges and universities frequently provide career-related classes—both credit and noncredit. They also maintain career centers for contacts and assessments.

- Shadowing or interviewing someone, as well as volunteering in the field that interests you, can be very valuable.

CONNECTING AND
COLLABORATING WITH OTHERS

Researching career options that match one's success criteria and Meaning Magnets requires solid information from multiple sources: the Internet, published material, and conversations and interactions with those actively involved in the work you believe to have meaning for you. All sources should be used in a synergistic process to discover what works best, fits your authentic self, and has the potential to provide a meaningful purpose you can pursue with a passion.

To really understand a career, you need to find people who are what you believe you want to become. Communicate, connect, volunteer, intern—do what it takes to make contact with them and their work in a positive and resourceful way. *The art of linking and networking is absolutely necessary for capitalizing on chaos.*

Albert Barabási says a lot on the cover of his book *Linked: The New Science of Networks—How Everything Is Connected to Everything Else and What It Means for Science, Business and Everyday Life!* (2002). We are all connected—everything touches everything—our world's biological systems, social worlds, economies, and religious traditions all tell a compelling story of interrelationships and connections. Barabási uses the example of Paul—responsible for the spread of Christianity—whom he called the world's first and greatest networker and salesperson. Paul walked 10,000 miles in twelve years, not aimlessly or randomly, but with a powerful purpose.

CONNECTING WITH THE WHOLE

Many people today feel lost, overwhelmed by conflicting demands, too much information, and rapid change. They see themselves in a system over which they have little control and of which they have little understanding. *The Fifth Discipline* (1990), by Peter Senge, focuses on chaos and complexity and the loss of purpose that comes in its wake. We have fragmented the world and lost connection with the whole.

Senge says that we must stop seeing the organization as a machine and see it as a kind of living organism. Systems thinking is Senge's "fifth discipline." It is the ability to understand the key interrelations that influence behavior in complex systems over time—seeing wholeness, not isolated parts. Systems thinking involves seeing through complexity to the underlying structure and patterns generating change. This requires a holistic approach that has integrity. Holistic systems thinking and planning are absolutely critical for effective, successful career management.

UNDERSTANDING THE
CHANGING WORK WORLD

Ralph Stacy (1996, p. 282), who extensively researched complexity in organizations, talks about the speed of change in organizations being faster than ever and the level of complexity being greater. He says that to contain the anxiety of creative activity in the midst of this complexity, we must learn to make sense of our experience of life within the organization, and the way we feel about it.

For a taste of all the radical shifts and changes in business careers, just leaf through Tom Peters' last four books. *Re-Imagine* (2003), his latest, is anything but a traditional business book, even though he is without question a leader in corporate management. The evolving chaos/complexity theory is extremely valuable in trying to grasp what Peters is teaching and how he is approaching it.

To understand what's out there that is a match for you, you must become aware of the reality of and changes in the workplace. This includes knowing about the large for-profit corporate organizations, smaller entrepreneurial start-ups, the PICs (professional independent contracting/consulting), and the nonprofits. People frequently are so focused on their own career niche situation and environment that they are scarcely aware of what is happening throughout the working environment. To understand and develop a plan for career success in today's workplace, it is imperative to become aware of how corporate organizations are handling today's change, and what is happening as a result.

Death of Certainty

In the quote at the beginning of this chapter, Mort Meyerson describes what we are experiencing as the "death of certainty"—that we can't assume that the immediate or long-term future of the work world will mirror or reflect the past, either for employees or for employers. With the current worldwide turbulence, growing complexity, and radical change plowing through every industry and altering management practices, predictability is impossible. Frankly, our intuitive, educated guesses based on possibilities and probabilities may be the best bet; this is a far cry from our organizational and management rules of the past.

The world as we know it is going away—this is the Age of Uncertainty and this will not change. Complexity, chaos, and insecurity in our work lives will continue. Workers must get used to constant change and learning, and this is our greatest challenge.

We have arrived at what Intel chairman Andrew Grove calls a "strategies infliction point." In *Only the Paranoid Survive* (1997), he describes a time in the life of a business or industry when the fundamentals are about to change or have done so already. That change can mean an opportunity to rise to new heights, or it may just as likely signal the beginning of the end.

In viewing today's capitalism, L. C. Thurow (1996, p. 7) borrows the term *punctuated equilibrium* from evolutionary biology to describe what he sees happening. This is very sudden change in an environment, when what has been dominant quickly disappears and a new species appears to replace it. Evolution then takes a quantum leap to another level. Ilya Prigogine's work also talks about this process, in which natural selection, which normally works on the margins, suddenly alters the core of the system. The dinosaurs that dominated the earth for 130 million years but suddenly disappeared are an example. Very real changes begin on the edges but can flip quickly to center stage. This is where we are in the work world today around the globe—the unusual happenings become the usual, and certainty becomes uncertainty and ambiguity.

"It's not just you and your company. The entire corporate world seems to be going crazy as companies cut costs but demand more," according to John Huey (1933, p. 38). The mission seems to be to keep everything running with increasing profits, while changing everything! In other words, the challenge is designing the new while operating the old. When researching the reality of a career, you cannot count on what it was in the past.

Call it re-engineering, restructuring, transformation, flattening, downsizing, right-sizing—the quest for global competitiveness is real, radical, and immediate. When it hits, it hurts. Urgency, fear, and uncertainty strike the ranks. To the survivors of all the corporate retrenching, the revolution feels scary, painful, liberating, disorienting, exhilarating, empowering, frustrating, fulfilling, confusing, and challenging—all at the same time! In other words, it's chaotic.

Reinventing Ourselves, Benjamin Franklin Style

Benjamin Franklin provides us with an excellent model of how to deal with change. He was a scientist, inventor, diplomat, writer, business strategist, and homespun humorist; he was also an ambitious urban entrepreneur, launching civic improvements such as a lending library and volunteer fire department, and a matching-grant fund-raiser. Franklin invented and continually reinvented himself to fit the need.

End of Scientific Command and Control

Frederick Taylor's *The Principles of Scientific Management* (1911) laid out an understandable, predictable, controllable system, an approach that was pure reductionism. Everything could be broken down into isolated parts in order to control them. Everything had to be neat and orderly.

People exploring career realities today must realize that organizations are moving to a more collaborative way of operating. In the 1950s, no-nonsense, control-from-the-top management was the norm. The organization took care of its employees, who were rarely encouraged to show initiative. The older, traditional scientific approach to management ensured control and promised to provide managers with the capacity to analyze, predict, and direct the behavior of the complex organizations they led. But the world that most managers now inhabit often appears to be unpredictable, uncertain, and even uncontrollable. The new imperative for the organization and employees is making sense of chaos.

Global Issues and Wild Cards

On global issues and changes in the workplace, Mary O'Hara Devereaux, director of research at the Institute of the Future Think Tank in California and coauthor of *Global Work* (1994), points out that all of us need to be futurists, and though we can't predict the future, we can characterize it. In a 1997 speech at the International Career Conference in San Jose, based on her extensive global experience, Devereaux stressed the following key trends affecting the workplace:

- Most companies today are only just beginning to become global. In the future, most companies will be global. So we must become culturally knowledgeable.

- Distance and place don't matter anymore in our technological world.

- China will have the largest workforce in the world in ten years, and technology in China is now second only to the United States.

- From 1995 to 2010 we will be working in a continuous clash: the Old World of hierarchical command and control culture versus the New World of emerging global cultures with team-based superordinate values.

- Demographics and longevity are two critical forces worldwide.

- In 2010, people in emerging countries will be half of the middle-class consumers, and this will transform our world. For instance, Proctor & Gamble says that in five years it will be selling three times more to the Chinese than to the U.S. marketplace.

- Rising bright stars of the future are in Asia. In twenty years, half of the world's labor force will be in Asia.

- Companies will outsource unskilled labor; jobs are not going away; skilled labor will be short, and many new types of service jobs are evolving.

In 1994, Devereaux stated that wild-card events, with a less than 5 percent chance of happening, were indeed occurring: the remodeling of immigration laws, the escalation of terrorism worldwide, stock market crashes. In the years since Devereaux's talk, we have experienced nothing but wild cards, or so it seems!

Chaos and Wild Cards in Raymond's Financial Career

I had been a successful professional in the investment field for twenty years—first an investment newsletter writer with a good reputation; then a successful stockbroker, achieving the senior vice president level at two major Wall Street firms. I had developed an expertise in managing money in the foreign currency market and had earned very large returns for my clients over many years. Then during the initial years of the Clinton administration, total chaos erupted in the currency markets. Over a two-year period the Swiss franc, the German mark, the Japanese yen—all the major currencies began to plunge and soar in unpredictable patterns. Trillions of dollars were lost, and my clients' accounts began to register losses rather than gains.

I had spent literally thousands of hours studying and mastering these markets, only to find that nothing I had come to understand meant anything anymore. Extreme chaotic movements became daily events—totally unpredictable and devastating to the fortunes of currency investors. My clients had become my friends, and I had earned their trust and respect over the years by making them excellent profits. Now these relationships were threatened (at least in my mind), and I fell into a long, deep depression that lasted for several years. My clients who invested in stocks and mutual funds continued to do well, but the large, successful currency business, which provided 90 percent of my income, was being methodically destroyed.

I had said for years that I would not be self-serving and that if the time came that I couldn't help people, I would quit rather than hurt them. I was almost fifty years old and had the resources to retire if I wanted to. I felt like I was a deeply troubled person who hadn't enjoyed life in years and I was ready to quit my job. My friends said I would be crazy to resign from my current position as senior vice president at my brokerage firm. They assured me that anyone would kill to have that job. But I was so unhappy that I was determined to get out of the investment business into something else or retire.

The idea that chaos is and always will be the norm but that there is order to be found in the chaos provided a new framework for approaching things. I realized that we all involve ourselves in useless attempts to avoid change and the unknown when we should embrace and look for the opportunities in the maelstrom. I thought of the times I had been hiking in the mountains in Oregon and had come to huge, house-sized boulders in a river. When the river was low, beautiful smooth patterns could be seen in the boulders where the rushing river had eroded natural works of art. I could imagine the total chaos of a rain-filled, thundering river resulting in these smooth, orderly, aesthetically pleasing patterns in the rocks. Nature, like all of life, was chaotic but produced and contained orderly forms.

So I determined that I would not expect the future to be anything like the past, but, rather, I would watch the increasingly rapid changes taking place in the world and look for the patterns within the chaos for ways to exploit and enjoy the changes. My job was not to hope things would stay the same or to battle to maintain the status quo (an impossible task) but to watch the changing rivers and get in the flow. Even better, I could absorb information each day and try to anticipate which way the economy, the job picture, and the demand for goods and services would go.

If I retired, I would basically live by investing in the stock market. I had acquired a skill level at investments that was higher than that of anyone I knew. I had a many-year history of making 15 to 20 percent on investments while sidestepping the brunt of every single major downdraft in the stock market. But I began to think about what a waste it would be to use my skills just to help myself when I could also help others.

I realized that I still loved working with investments and had an affinity with numbers and systems, but I didn't want to work within the confines and under the pressures of a major brokerage firm anymore. So I started my own investment business, no longer working with foreign currencies. I would concentrate on helping people with stock and mutual fund investments.

I began this new business at the worst possible time . . . the end of 1999. Within months the worst bear market since the Great Depression began—a three-year-long slide that erased a decade's worth of gains. Most people's investment holdings dropped 50 to 60 percent. All the rules I had learned about investing were savaged. Fortunately, I took almost all of my clients' money out of the market. Historically, when the Federal Reserve had dropped interest rates two to three times, the stock market would go up at an 18.9 percent rate of return. This time the Federal Reserve dropped rates ten times, battling the downward spiral, and the market just kept plummeting: chaos again.

I fell into a new wave of depression. First the currency market had self-destructed, now the stock market. I found it very difficult to detach myself and look for the order within the chaos. Mentally I railed against the injustice of having two businesses implode back-to-back. The only positive was that I was getting a modicum of new business from people who had heard from my clients that I had shielded their accounts from big losses.

So I went back to the drawing board to try to determine what I should have learned from the chaos in order to get a quicker read on the next round. What I found astounded me. Despite the weak economy, with mortgage rates so low, thousands moved out of apartments and built their first homes. People who already had homes built bigger ones. I saw that, during the three-year 50 percent drop in the stock market, homebuilding stocks went up about 200 percent. One, NVR, increased more than 700 percent.

Another example: Symantec, a software company fighting computer viruses, tripled. With thousands of people out of work, companies in the business of reeducating adults for new jobs saw their profits growing 50 percent or more per year. Their stocks increased 150 percent. Certain drug companies and health benefit managers grew dramatically. With the population aging and health costs soaring, owners of health-care stocks had enjoyed profits of more than 150 percent.

I devised a way to use a computer to spot any such trends in any industry in the future. My goal was to make it impossible for stocks of growing, appreciating companies to escape my attention. I created a computer radar screen that I would monitor every day. It would interpret chaos by combing through thousands of stocks to find those companies whose profits were growing and whose stocks were increasing in value. I wanted to find stocks that went up no matter what the economy or the rest of the stock market was doing. In short, I found a way to find order and opportunity in a thundering, chaotic river.

But my understanding of chaos theory says not to depend on the future being like the past. Just because almost every year has seen a major up-move in stocks, bonds, or gold doesn't mean that that pattern will continue. So I've devised a way to use computers to spot persistent patterns of appreciation in technology, oil, biotechnology, health care, real estate, and many other markets. My job, as I see it, is not to predict the future but to read what is happening, to believe what I'm seeing, and to put my clients' investments in tune with the flow.

Now my business is finally becoming profitable. While I'm not out of the woods, my income doubled last year, and I'm seeing a steady stream of new business, mainly coming from referrals by existing clients. I can definitely see a light at the end of the tunnel.

In retrospect I see that I wasted years in the "long dark night," as I was overwhelmed by the massive adverse changes in the U.S. and world economies. It didn't help that I wasted mental energy bemoaning the seeming unfairness of the things that happened to me. Now as I drive to my office each morning, I listen to the news and I force myself to think about what new changes may be at hand or just over the horizon. I assess current patterns and detect new ones. Without the use of a computer I think it would be impossible to survey the information flows and detect new trends. Reading, thinking, and using the computer for detective work are, I think, essential for anyone who wants to find order in the chaos. So my advice would be to stop bemoaning change and learn to embrace it and exploit its opportunities. We all need to see life as an ever-changing adventure to which we must constantly adapt ourselves. I recently found a fortune cookie message that says it all: Life is like a poker game; you're always getting dealt a new hand.

SEVEN

Looking Forward

At every crossroads on the way that leads to the future,
each progressive spirit is opposed by a thousand men
appointed to guard the past.

—MAURICE MAETERLINCK

After looking inward through a variety of self-assessment processes to gain authentic awareness, then looking outward for information about the challenges, needs, and opportunities in the external world, the next step is looking forward—coordinating the internal and the external into a coherent vision. The making of meaning for career success on the edge of chaos requires vision—a creative but reality-based future image of ourselves actually involved in a career that matches the Meaning Magnets, our success criteria, our authentic self, with the demands of the external environment. Vision can solve a specific problem, and it can also help us discover our possibilities, our next steps.

It is critical to have a deep authentic sense of yourself so that the vision is not confined to a narrow passage. As we move forward in life, we discover meaningful jobs to be done and needs to be filled, based on our instinctive Meaning Magnets. This helps us reframe past "failures" as "lessons learned," the basic raw material for the art of becoming the authentic self. Our imaginations can tyrannize or liberate us. We are not so much run by what happens as by what we expect. Drop the fear of failure and our vision of the future becomes a state of mind—a way of remembering the future, moving toward a target that the culture has perhaps not yet articulated but can be perceived by those who are sensitive. In *The Fifth Discipline* (1990), Peter Senge states, "Truly creative people use the gap between vision and current reality to generate energy for change" (p. 153).

DISCOVERING OUR VISION FOR THE FUTURE

It is imperative in our crisis of uncertainty that we consciously create, cultivate, and utilize our vision for the future. We must actually see our future vision in the mind's eye, and use it in our thinking and planning. Our vision must be tied to larger issues in society and must recognize what will nourish our authentic self.

The capacity to see or sense the possible and to see how to get there is the mechanism for individual evolution as well as social progress. In the course of fulfilling a vision we re-envision ourselves as well—what we might be as well as what we might do.

Visionary Action

To discover our future vision, we must create mental images—important successful actions in our mind's eye. This isn't casual daydreaming; it's taking visionary action. We are told that imagined events, conceived and held in the mind's eye, are recorded by the brain. Commitment to the truth of ourselves is important for developing subconscious rapport. When we don't tell ourselves the truth, we create noise and distraction, "chatter" that creates bodily stress—for the subconscious this is ultimately negative. This is the principle for the operation of lie detectors: untruth results in the activation of stress.

The subconscious—a part of the mind that is exceedingly capable of dealing with complexity—operates below or behind conscious awareness. The subconscious operates most effectively when we are clearly focused on our vision and our current reality. Imaging and visualizing are important techniques for focusing the subconscious. When we are unclear, the subconscious has no way of prioritizing and focusing.

Mental rehearsal must be based absolutely on our own truth—on *knowing what we really want*. However, we must learn to separate what we want from what we think we want or ought to want. One's genuine aspirations are central. The subconscious is especially receptive to goals in line with deeper values and aspirations. A strict reliance only on conscious learning and input will make it difficult to achieve the highest level.

Vision goes far beyond merely seeing and avoiding the holes in the road. It anticipates needs and possibilities beyond the norm and beyond the present. Vision is the pilot function, an ability to grasp the larger picture—the world beyond one's particular road. It enables us to do what has to be done, even if we have never done it before and even if no one has ever done it before. If our society is to make it through the present turbulence with any grace at all, we have no sensible choice but to cultivate vision.

Authentic Focus

What do you truly care about? For lasting career success and satisfaction, you must know what you see as your mission—your purpose based on what you care about and can become committed to. Determining and sticking to a commitment based on the authentic self is difficult, because we don't anticipate the demands, and the fear of missing out on other things causes us to leap from one attraction of the false self to another.

A future vision that is passionately valued brings forth genius and talents you were unaware you possessed. And it is this fulfilling vision that binds us to pursuit of our purpose, a plan that organizes our intelligence and lights our fire.

The Creative Vision That Comes from Chaos

Thomas Paine once said, "There is existing in [us] a mass of sense lying in a dormant state, and which, unless something excites it to action, will descend with [us], in that condition, to the grave."

When we have a vision of who we intend to become, we can reconstruct the personality around it. Robert Assagioli (1965, p. 21) calls this process psychosynthesis. It involves a vision that distinguishes the true self (the authentic self) from other elements that control the personality (the false self) and forms the personality around it.

Commitment

Living by our future vision requires commitment to mission and purpose. Commitment demands carefully considered creative risk taking, decision making that is not about merely pleasing others, and looking to the authentic self rather than mindlessly following authority figures or role models. It may call for performing some tasks that one would prefer not to; commitment may shift as we mature, achieve, and reassess our mission, and this limits options—we can't have it all since we have only so much time and energy in life. We must know where we want to go and how to get there.

Cultivating Creativity and Intuition

It is important to understand the nature of both creativity and intuition involved in this process of envisioning the future. (These are discussed in detail later in this chapter.) Having a future vision based on the authentic self and a congruent opportunity in the work world fires us up and provides the fuel for creating a plan for the passionate pursuit of purpose. However, many of us, long feeling boxed in or trapped in an ill-fitting career, must sharpen, release, and develop our intuition and creativity before we can begin to visualize future images. Liberating these is a significant part of the career design process.

One of the greatest challenges in discovering our vision for the future is trying to make sense out of nonsense, putting together the disparate, disconnected pieces of our world into some perspective and developing harmony out of the chaos we are experiencing. It takes the Type CC (change catalyst) personality to use creativity and intuition in a time of chaos. The Type CC personality takes a present and future perspective and frequently makes sound judgment based on intuition and instinct.

Changing Our Luck

Daniel Pink (2003, p. 79) writes that in an environment of rising tensions and diminished expectations, most of us could use some luck—personally, professionally, and financially—to go with our creativity. He interviewed Richard Wiseman, head of the Psychology Research Department at the University of Hertfordshire in England and author of *The Luck Factor: Changing Your Luck, Changing Your Life* (Miramax, 2003). For eight years, Wiseman has studied what makes people lucky, and he claims that he has broken the code. It isn't kismet, karma, or coincidence—lucky people, without knowing it, think and behave differently.

Psychology has avoided the subject of luck because it isn't "scientific," but Wiseman has built a database. Pink (2003, p. 79) summarizes Wiseman's four principles of luck:

- Maximize chance opportunities.

- Listen to your lucky hunches—stay open to possibilities (what I call using your third eye and third ear).

- Expect good fortune (the Norman Vincent Peale approach).

- Turn bad luck into good.

There is a distinction between chance and luck. Chance is like winning the lottery—no control other than buying the ticket. When people have consistent good fortune, their luck can be attributed to something they are doing. They are open to new experiences, not routine. They risk and relax enough to see opportunity. Unlucky people are stuck in routines; lucky people want something new. The reality is that we have more control than we thought we had.

How else do lucky people's minds work differently? They practice counterfactual thinking, which is automatic and unconscious. The degree to which you think that something is fortunate or not is the degree to which you generate alternatives that are better or worse! There's no bad luck to the lucky person, according to Wiseman.

The Vision Quest

We can think of our vision quest as a tradition of renewal. We leave all behind—the community, its structure, and our own customary perceptions. We are searching for a part of ourselves that has been obscured by our habits and history. We look outward across new vistas, we look inward for new images, and we look forward to carrying our vision back to others. This is what many experience in the career change process. If we relate the story of our journey and what was life altering for us to others, we communicate the learned vision. Activity 5 will help you visualize your future.

Vision Quests of American Indians

Vision quests were traditionally undertaken by tribal leaders or young males as a rite of passage. The individual would leave all behind and go alone and without food to a mountaintop, canyon, or other remote site and would not return to the tribe until he had a mystical experience, often involving an encounter with an animal.

ACTIVITY 5: Envisioning the Future

Envisioning your future self can release desires and talents that you have not yet tapped into fully. Contemplate the following questions and answer them without restraint.

- *What would you like to be an expert in or known for?*

- *Imagine that a great crowd has gathered to meet you. What would you like someone to say in introducing you?*

- *What is your personal mission statement—your purpose in life? How do you want others to remember you?*

- *List your desires, talents, skills, strengths, and motivations that will help you gain this purpose.*

- *List the negatives and weaknesses that stand in your way of accomplishing this.*

- *How can you activate this mission or purpose? What future actions must you take?*

- *What specific actions can you take now and in the future? List what you can do immediately (within a month) and what you can do within one year.*

Visualize yourself five years from now. Either write or draw (your choice, and you don't have to be an artist) a description of your situation in detail—where you live, what you do and where, what you do in your leisure time, how you dress, who you communicate with and on what, and what you enjoy most about your life.

CREATIVITY AS THE FOUNDATION FOR CAREER VISION

Success in agrarian times required land; in the Industrial Age, money and muscle created wealth; and the Information Age requires knowledge and brains. But we are moving into an age of innovation, in which success will require creativity and imagination. Innovation will be the engine of this economic movement (see Esther Dyson's 1997 book *Release 2.0: A Design for Living in the Digital Age*). The constant flow of new ideas and technology is the key: The most successful will be those who can design innovations to help the company get or stay ahead.

Creativity is a feat of mental gymnastics engaging the conscious and subconscious parts of the brain. It draws on knowledge, logic, imagination, intuition, and the ability to see connections and to use different modes of thought. Employees will increasingly need to be good at thinking rather than blindly following routine. Be aware that skills for career success in the age of innovation are almost totally different from those required for the Industrial Age. Then, you were successful based on your talent for figuring out what your boss wanted and passively plugging away.

Can we leap into the future without a detailed road map and formulas, without the encouragement of the masses behind us? That depends on whether we have the courage to move creatively ahead, in spite of the pain and fear we may be experiencing at the edge of chaos.

Creativity in Work and Life

Creativity is the ability to transcend traditional conventional ideas, rules, patterns, and relationships and to create meaningful new ideas, forms, methods, and interpretations. Determining one's meaning and purpose is a highly creative process and an integral part of finding the real self.

Creativity is an extension of one's self, requiring effort and struggle and the willingness to endure anxiety, since creative efforts have the potential to fail, to be critiqued unfavorably, or to be rejected by others. When people are unwilling to risk, they forgo creative endeavors for their future and make peace with living below their career potential. Creativity does not come easy—even to those with much talent. There is always risk and much work involved.

Creative thinking Follow the rules, be practical, always have the right answer, relax, avoid stress, don't judge, don't fail, be original, do it perfectly! Michael Michalko (2003) points out that in the past we have been taught rigid reproductional thinking for solving problems, instead of productively thinking of new and different ways to solve problems. He sees the biggest obstacle to innovative thinking to be that we are taught *what to think instead of how to think*. Michalko (p. 55) introduces the idea of blending, which puts dissimilar concepts together—but only those that your unconscious mind connects to—to form a new one. He cautions that expertise and knowledge can create a kind of conceptual inertia that inhibits and constrains creative thought in science, art, and industry.

Creativity in schools The work of Howard Gardner in *Frames of Mind* (1983) and *Multiple Intelligences* (1993) stresses that there are multiple and different intelligences and different areas of strength. Our culture has traditionally placed more value on some and disregarded others. For example, the academic world has routinely ignored the major strengths of many students by teaching primarily to the linear, analytical, and verbal intelligences and skills, as opposed to the conceptual, creative, and intuitive. This failure to honor these various intelligences is a component of our school system all the way through the graduate level. Yet these intuitive and interpersonal skills are becoming increasingly important. Many adults are scurrying to acquire them, and many are unwittingly being penalized, both personally and professionally, for not using them.

Traditionally, business schools have not stressed creativity but have taught people to frame problems, formulate alternatives, collect data, and evaluate opinions. Michael Ray, however, a professor at Stanford Business School, started teaching a course on creativity in the late 1970s and cowrote a book (Ray and Myers, 1989) in which he summarizes five fundamentals of creativity.

- Creativity is essential for succeeding in business and life.

- Everyone is creative.

- Ego, chatter of the mind, and fear of judgment knock down many before they begin.

- Stay aware of your creativity, use "flow," and operate "in the zone."

- Creativity is idiosyncratic; find your own particular way. There are no formulas.

Creative personalities often enjoy the discussion of cutting-edge ideas. According to Emily Smith (1985, p. 82), studies have shown that advanced education only rarely helps and may actually squelch creativity.

Creativity and the dark night Creativity may assume many different forms, and while stress can have a negative effect in that more stress equals less creativity, a bout with depression may bring creativity. Jung said that in his long periods of falling apart, in a "state of disorientation" as he called it, he conceived some of his fundamental psychological insights. In other words, creativity finds its soul when it embraces its shadow.

Creative work can be exciting, inspiring, and godlike, but according to Thomas Moore (1992), it is also quotidian, humdrum, and full of anxieties, frustrations, dead ends, mistakes, and failures: "We may get to a point where our external labors and opus of the soul are one and the same, inseparable. Then the satisfaction of our work will be deep and long-lasting, undone neither by failure nor by flashes of success" (p. 199).

Often, accomplishing a major goal or making creative leaps is preceded by a chaotic time of struggle. In capitalizing on career chaos, we need to realize that the chaos of change is neither bad nor to be totally avoided, but it is to be used as a signal that perhaps creativity and renewal are in progress. Something new on a higher level may well be beginning to evolve. Don't squeeze it out, but ask yourself if a creative birth is about to take place inside you. When in our need for order we stop the chaos or close it off, we may be interrupting the process of growth. Creative change, the move to a higher level, is a process that proceeds at its own pace.

Creativity Blocks

What keeps us from using our naturally creative selves?

Loss of instinct　The former career security system, emphasizing mechanism, reductionism, determinism, and linearity, came at a high price. We lost our instinct for personal survival—traded it off for what we presumed to be long-term certainty and security.

Yet silencing our survival instincts and intuition is now having serious repercussions. We're strangers to ourselves, and we don't see how we can live without all the former beliefs of certainty and external trappings, even though millions in the workplace are carrying a cavity of meaninglessness in their souls. We've surrendered much of our personal independence and the willingness to creatively embrace a new challenge. We settled for the tyranny of the prescribed formula and devoted ourselves to maintaining an established, but woefully outdated, system that now has ceased to support us.

Now many feel trapped on a treadmill, existing mainly to keep the mindless, outdated machine system working. Many passed up opportunities, traded off self-confidence and became like passive, dependent children; now many harbor the deep-seated fear that they cannot handle the adversity and uncertainty of major change. Now what many see ahead for themselves, their children, and their grandchildren is sobering and dim, if not downright dark. We misjudge and mistrust our instincts and intuition and they lie idle from nonuse.

Avoidance One of the most common problems in being creative is avoidance—the need to protect oneself from the anxiety and depression that the creative process can cause. People commonly say, "I would like to make a career change, but . . . ," and so on, and so on. The "yes, but" syndrome is like a thick wall that is almost impossible to move beyond.

Incorrectly defining creativity Creativity is often mistakenly limited to artistic expression such as writing, painting, dancing, or music. Yet there is another kind of creativity that has little if anything to do with this kind of artistic talent or output. James Masterson (1988) explains it as "the personal creativity of the real self that can make original, unique and effective arrangements of one's interior life, which are, in turn, expressed outwardly in new, more adaptive and harmonious ways of living" (p. 229). This involves the remaking of inner psychological patterns—images, feelings, values, and thoughts—that can then be given outward expression to shape one's environment, activities, and relationships. Moore (1992) advocates bringing the idea of creativity down to earth, not reserving it for exceptional individuals or brilliance. "In ordinary life, creativity means making something for the soul out of every experience" (p. 198).

Creativity is also commonly mistaken for total originality. Some people say, "I can't create anything original, but I can take pieces and ideas that someone else has and put them together in a better way." And they launch into a description of an innovative project they've completed, without having seen their actions as creative at all. Many people think like this, seeing creativity as being able to do something entirely new and different. But it is also a creative act to take existing facts and ideas and combine and synthesize them in a different way into a new product or idea without following the ordinary rules.

Early Creativity Loss

The suppression of creativity begins when we are young. As children, we are more creative than we realize; but, unfortunately, research shows that a child's creativity plummets 90 percent between the ages of five and seven—the sad reality is that school can be detrimental. By age forty, most adults are only 2 percent as creative as they were at age five, as reported by Emily Smith (1985, p. 81).

Creativity and the Authentic Self

In *Love, Medicine, and Miracles* (1986), Bernie Siegel says, "Becoming your own person releases your creativity. . . . Freed from bonds of convention and the fear of what others may think, the mind responds with new solutions, new goals. . . . You become able to take risks, to experiment with your own life" (p. 168). He also stresses that those who develop their full individuality can find opportunity to live inventively in their work. They can change jobs and move from a secure career that is boring to one that brings meaning.

Masterson (1988) stresses that the fully developed real self always has access to its creativity. The birthright of the real self is creativity, the ability to invent or to rearrange old patterns in new ways. "Everyone with a healthy real self has the potential for leading a creative life and dealing with problems and challenges in innovative ways" (p. 208).

Descriptions of Creativity and the Creative Process

Rollo May: The birth of something new

Carl Rogers: The ability to toy with elements and concepts . . . to play spontaneously with ideas, colors, shapes, relationships—to juggle, to juxtapose, to shape wild hypotheses— "brainstorming"—to express the ridiculous, to translate from one form to another

Eric Fromm: To consider the whole process of life as a process of birth, and not to take any stage of life as a final stage

Source: Adapted from McLeish, 1976, p. 34.

Research has identified dozens of characteristics of creativity. Activity 6 presents twelve of these to help you begin to examine your own creativity.

ACTIVITY 6: Creative Attributes

As an exploratory activity, rank yourself from 1 to 5 (5 being the highest) on the characteristics you have and value in your life and work. Are there any that you would like to cultivate for your future?

- *Capacity to be puzzled*
- *Awareness*
- *Spontaneity*
- *Spontaneous flexibility*
- *Adaptive flexibility*
- *Divergent thinking*
- *Openess to new experience*
- *Disregard of boundaries*
- *Abandoning*
- *Letting go*
- *Being born every day*
- *Ability to toy with the elements*
- *Gusto (relish) for temporary chaos*
- *Tolerance of ambiguity*

Source: Adapted from Anderson ,1959.

USING OUR INTUITION

Intuition is a higher form of mind than what we call "thinking." It embraces the functions of both the left and the right brain. It includes the wisdom of the heart as well as logic. It's the knowledge of the "masculine" specific and the "feminine" connective. It asks what a thing is in itself and in its relationship to the whole; natural knowing doesn't have to choose between the two.

In *How to Think with Your Gut*, Thomas Stewart (2002) stresses that science is starting to understand why best decisions—tough calls under pressure—come from the gut rather than a detailed master plan. In a fluid, competitive environment, the best decisions come from intuition, which is intelligence and understanding that bypasses the logical, linear cognitive process. It is the faculty of direct knowing, as if by instinct, without conscious reasoning: pure, untaught inferential knowledge with a keen and quick insight and common sense. The use of intuition is becoming more recognized in the business world. Starbucks' CEO Howard Schultz emphasizes that the "most brilliant decisions come from the gut" (quoted in Stewart 2002, p. 99).

On the Value of Intuition

"My intuition was not strong enough in the field of mathematics to differentiate clearly the fundamentally important . . . from the rest of the more or less dispensable erudition. Also, my interest in the study of nature was no doubt stronger. . . . In this field I soon learned to scent out that which might lead to fundamentals and to turn aside . . . from the multitude of things that clutter up the mind and divert it from the essentials." —Albert Einstein

Knowing on a deeper level is like discovering a hidden picture. Sometimes lives can change in a flash with a blinding glimpse of the obvious. Natural knowing is intuitive knowing: "A natural knower understands by receiving knowledge from his or her total beingness as it interacts with all other beingness" (Karpinski 1990, p. 257).

Research is beginning to explain why a growing body of information from economics, neurology, cognitive psychology, and other fields suggests that intuition or instinct, hunch, "learning without awareness" is a real form of knowledge. It may seem nonrational, but it involves processing more information and on a higher level than formerly dreamed of.

Role of Intuition in Decision Making

Psychologists say intuition is inseparable from decision making. Stewart (2002) stresses that "in complex or chaotic situations—a battlefield, a trading floor, or today's brutally competitive business environment—intuition usually beats rational analysis. And as science looks closer, it is coming to see that intuition is not a gift, but a skill that can be learned" (p. 100).

Stewart describes the research of cognitive psychologist Gary Klein, who studied U. S. marines under pressure. Klein compared the marines with a group of stock traders, both on the floor and in a simulated battlefield environment. In both environments, the traders thoroughly trounced the marines. The conclusion was that the traders were the better gut thinkers: They make quick decisions and act decisively on imperfect and contradictory information. Today, the official Marine Corps doctrine reads, "The intuitive approach is more appropriate for the vast majority of . . . decisions made in the fluid, rapidly changing conditions of war when time and uncertainty are critical factors and creativity is a desirable trait" (in Stewart 2002, p. 101).

The old decision-making approach The old way of making decisions (see Klein 2003) was to

1. Analyze problems thoroughly

2. List alternatives

3. Evaluate options based on your decision criteria

4. Rank criteria in importance

5. Rate each criteria

6. Do the math

7. Pick the one with the highest score

This is thorough, systematic, rational, and scientific. Gary Klein (2003, p. 10), however, says this is a myth. It doesn't work in the real world, where there is challenge, confusion, complexity, inconclusive information, short time, and high stakes. Most life decisions today are not amenable to the traditional decision-making approach.

Avoiding analysis paralysis Behind many errors in decision making is a yearning for the "right answers"—if only we could examine enough data and know all the alternatives. Finding rules to supply all the answers is not possible, in business and everywhere else, and people get caught in "analysis paralysis" and prolonged procrastination. "Command and control management went out with tail-fins. Risks are both greater and less predictable . . . More and more all you can do is admit that you simply don't know and go with your gut" (Stewart 2002, p. 104). No one likes uncertainty, but when surrounded by it, our gut may have something important to say to us! To tap into our gut instincts, we sometimes need to get out of our own way, and trust those instincts.

Balancing Intuition with Analysis

It is clear that intuition plays an essential role in decision making. However, Eric Bonabean (2003) cautions that intuition alone "can be dangerously unreliable in complicated situations" (p. 116). He emphasizes that the more complex the situation, the more misleading intuition becomes in a truly chaotic environment, when cause and effect have no linear relationship.

On the edge of chaos, we must balance intuition with analysis. We must learn to leverage instinct without being sabotaged by its weakness. Klein (2003) recommends that we start with intuition, not analysis—balance the two out, and don't agonize over a perfect choice. This balancing act is a talent we must learn in order to solve career problems and to succeed on the edge of chaos. Activity 7 focuses further on your creativity and innovation traits to help you with your balancing act.

ACTIVITY 7: Creativity and Innovation Checklist

Review these creativity/innovation traits and put a check mark beside the ones that reflect your usual habits. Those that aren't checked reveal areas to expand for greater creativity.

Choice: *Changing states or rhythms and moving dynamically*

Dropping: *Letting go of a fixed position*

Flexibility: *Expanding and contracting*

Imagination: *Generating images and/or ideas*

Initiative: *Starting and moving from intention to action*

Noticing: *Detecting changes and scanning environment for new relationships*

Probing: *Moving into new experiences with flexibility, tentativeness, curiosity*

Purpose: *Passionately pursuing a mission*

Recovery: *Regaining composure after a perceived failure*

Reframing: *Moving to a new perspective—rearranging and adding to the known*

Risking: *Freeing self from fear of failure*

Story: *Seeing and communicating circumstances and meaning*

Timing: *Avoiding premature or too-late action and closure*

Tuning: *Sensing the fixed details and agendas*

Vitality: *Having energy for exploring, risking, recovering*

While many clients are somewhat systematic and analytical in coming up with their future vision, others take a more creative approach. Let Kitty tell you how she discovered her vision. Highly creative in art, painting, and writing, a former professional singer, she became a corporate wife by working her husband's way through college as a secretary. After he became financially successful, Kitty, now a single parent, focused on rearing two highly talented children and started a children's theater. I went to several of her annual Christmas parties that were attended by so many that I thought she could easily be elected mayor of her suburban city! She describes the internal process of making her decision to move on and pick up her creative business. She has now moved to New York and is highly successful and satisfied in her art, writing, and music. I received an e-mail from her while she was in the decision-making process.

Kitty's Creative Search for Her Future Vision

Just when we think it can't be said again, another voice comes forward out of the darkness, and this is the voice that speaks our language. I have read hundreds of books and attended dozens of lectures, motivational meetings, and spiritual movements on career choices, on career crisis, about change and transition, and forward thinking. Every one of those books read, lectures attended, motivational meetings and spiritual movements studied offered something I could use. The incubation period lasted a long time for me.

I came to believe that I could meet my future vision of myself as an artist, and I began to make choices based on what I believed. If I believe in myself, then I trust my judgment, I see mistakes as experimentation, I rest easy in the knowledge that I can handle anything.

At first, when I tried to be myself, I was given all kinds of signals to be quiet, "sensible" reasons to not express myself, acceptable ways to hide my light. That is directly opposed to the nature of creativity. When I live in opposition to nature . . . my nature . . . I fail.

I live inside my days, enjoying the challenges, seeing life/change as a chance to make a new picture. When I paint, I sometimes spill a color I didn't intend to use. Instead of getting frustrated or angry and throwing it away, I step back and look at the spill as a part of the picture instead of a blotch on my perfectly planned idea. Always, without fail, the spill leads me to something more interesting, and ultimately beautiful.

EIGHT

Taking Action

As any change must begin somewhere, it is the single individual who will undergo it and carry it through. The change must begin with the individual: it might be any one of us. Nobody can . . . wait for someone else to do what he is loath to do himself.

—C. G. JUNG

Balancing life and career on the edge of chaos requires creative decision making and an action plan. Armed with knowledge of our success criteria and our Meaning Magnets, an awareness of the outer world, and our future vision, we can now fully initiate the fourth stage of our career design plan: taking action to reach our goals.

MOVING FROM VISUALIZATION TO REALIZATION

It's time to take stock of what you've done so far to create your career design plan. Activity 8 is designed for that purpose.

ACTIVITY 8: Summarizing Your Career Design Plan So Far

• *My Meaning Magnets that I can identify are*

• *My main skills and talents are*

• *My success criteria are*

• *Answers that I have gotten from others to my "Grail questions" include*

• *Things I have done so far to realize my vision for the future, and things I still plan to do, include*

• *Ways that I am using my creativity and innovation traits and attributes are*

Taking Action with Intentionality

Robert Assagioli (1973, p. 243), an Italian colleague of Freud, Jung, and Maslow, calls the will—intentionality—a responsible mover. He dismisses the older Victorian ideas about will as something stern and repressive used to force oneself into action contrary to natural drives. He shows how the will can be a constructive force that guides intuition, emotions, and imagination toward a complete realization of the self.

Assagioli stresses the wide gap between man's external and internal powers: "Man has had to pay dearly for his material achievement. His life has become richer, broader, and more stimulating, but at the same time more complicated and exhausting" (p. 4). The rapidly increasing tempo, myriad opportunities for gratifying desires, and intricate economic and social machinery have enmeshed us in more insistent demands on our energy, mental functions, emotions, and will. For evidence, just look at one typical day in your life. To achieve our future vision requires time for thought and faith in ourselves and our goals.

Assagioli (1973) stresses that "faith leading to a sense of certainty requires primarily faith in oneself, that is, in the real self, in what we are essentially" (p. 171). The true use of our will or intentionality requires synthesis of faith and connection and brings power, potency, and energy, yet the individual often lacks ability to deal with all this. To close the fatal gap, Assagioli (p. 6) recommends the simplification of our outer life and development of our inner power—exactly the opposite of what is experienced by so many today!

There are two reasons for tapping into the unrealized potency of the will:

- It has a central position in our personality and an intimate connection with the core of our being—the authentic self.

- It plays a key role in deciding what is to be done and in applying the necessary means for this realization.

Discovering the reality and nature of the will helps us achieve career success on the edge of chaos, as *meaningful purpose must be coupled with the will for action.* The neglect or misuse of the will is unfortunate because of the enormous potential inherent in its right use for achieving self-actualization and self-realization and for solving major career problems.

The will can also make skillful use of all the energies existing in the personality, that is, thinking and imagination, perception and intuition, feeling and impulse. "The will can move the body and evoke corresponding images and ideas, which in turn intensify the emotion and feelings it works to strengthen. In other words, through conscious and purposeful movement, one can evoke and strengthen positive and desired inner states" (Assagioli, p. 53). Ideas and images tend to awaken the emotions and feelings that correspond to them.

As we overcome personal and career uncertainties, we must have a purpose that creates enough intensity, or fire in our belly, to keep the will in action. Thankfully, this strength of will can be developed and increased through practice and exercise, but also we must work on the skillful will, which is the ability to develop the specific strategy that is most effective to gain a predetermined goal. In other words, it's essential to stay on a learning curve for what works best.

Six Stages to Realization of Our Goals

Assagioli (1973, pp. 138–139) provides six stages of intentionality for moving from visualization to realization. These steps are like links of a chain—all six links must stay strong as we take action to pursue our purpose. The stages as described here are adapted from his model.

Stage 1: Clear vision The first stage involves clear vision of our goal combined with our intention to achieve it. Our future vision is based on evaluation of our Meaning Magnets and our success criteria, based on our authentic self, combined with the reality of the external world. We need intention—zest and aroused drive to achieve— otherwise this discussion is academic only. Good intentions are not enough; they must be followed up wisely.

Stage 2: Deliberation The next stage involves deliberation. We must examine and consider all factors relevant to realization of our vision. We must be sure to include our unconscious motives. Our choices must be made by preference, by seeing clearly and using genuine foresight, inspiration, intuition, and discrimination.

Stage 3: Choice and decision This is the time to choose a given aim and set aside or discard others. Beware of indecision created by conflicts between conscious and unconscious motives, fear of making mistakes, or unwillingness to make mistakes. This requires foresight.

Stage 4: Focus In this stage we focus the energy and time needed to achieve the goal of our future vision. Establish volition and a state of certainty and resolution. Use affirmation—words of power in a calm, quiet, nonaggressive manner. Strive for a synthesis of faith and conviction. Avoid all hurry and impatience to see results.

Stage 5: Plan A careful plan and program, including our personal life, are needed—including means and phases of the execution of the plan through time, circumstances, and existing possibilities. Formulate clearly the goal to be reached and retain it unswervingly in mind through stages of execution. This is difficult but essential.

Stage 6: Directing the execution The proper function or specific task of the will is not to carry out the execution directly as commonly supposed, but to direct it. To use a theater analogy: The will is the director of the entire production but normally not one of the actors. This direction includes constant supervision of the execution. The will calls up the various functions needed for its purpose and provides instruction, direction, commands, and supervision. It oversees development of the program and ensures that it follows the right course. This involves a constant adaptation to changing conditions.

FIGHTING RESISTANCE TO CHANGE

Paradoxically, both a fear of knowing and a fear of not knowing arise when we change or take control of our careers. The fear revolves around an inner dialogue: "What will I discover if I find the real me? What if I don't like the me that I find? What if others don't like the real me? Who am I to think I can be different?" "What if I take this career decision making really seriously, but I don't succeed? Is it better not to know?" "If I never really try, I'll never have to know and face the worst—that I couldn't succeed no matter how hard I tried." All kinds of fears and questions surface at this time—like Pandora's box, maybe it's better to keep the lid closed. Better the devil I know than the devil I don't know! Jung says that these fears are so great that we may dare not even admit them to ourselves.

Are You in "Plato's Cave"?

In *The Republic* (1968), Plato spoke to the inability of people to take in information outside their usual belief systems. He relates the parable of people who lived in chains, facing the back wall of a dark cave. One escaped and came back and reported a miraculous outside world of light, color, and substance, and urged the others to join him. The prisoners thought he was crazy because the new information did not fit into their personal experience, and they refused to leave the cave.

Courage to be yourself—authentic fearlessness—is not the absence of fear, but the ability to meet whatever comes with curiosity and creativity. Turn negative fear into life-giving energy. The most important courageous step we can take is to give up who we think we *should be,* and do what it takes to be ourselves.

Many apparently successful men and women question their courage to take charge of their own careers and make the changes they long for. They can take risks and solve complicated, risky problems effectively in their jobs but have never considered using that same talent and ability to deal with their personal career needs. They have taken on and succeeded in all kinds of challenges for their company, even going to bat for their people and their projects, but they have not done this for themselves.

Why Can't You Do It?

One young lawyer put money above all else and was making $300,000 annually at a job in which his real talents did not fit. For six years he forced himself to do the work. Hit with panic attacks, he started seeing a therapist and began to realize that he was shortening his life. The point is this: If you can be successful in something you don't like or fit, just think how successful you could be in what you are passionate about!

When facing change and risk in their careers, many truly gifted people become almost mindless, devoid of any creative ideas or foresight. They behave like trapped animals in a psychologist's research lab—

fearful, thoughtless, clueless on understanding their options or even acknowledging that they have any. Their limited self-concept can't acknowledge options that extend to their own needs.

Turning Loose Self-Defeating Behavior

The turning loose of self-defeating behavior precedes the gaining of personal power, as facing and solving career issues creates a spiritual, emotional, and psychological skill-building process that unites all activities and concepts for determining and achieving career purpose. This can be seen as a transformation to the Type CC personality, which results in more creative control over a career for a lifetime.

Anytime we change, deeply change, from the inside out, we turn loose something that has been blocking us. We may have unconsciously held mistaken beliefs about ourselves, our needs, and the outer world that have caused us great difficulty. These wrong beliefs have occupied a center in our lives that we believed was absolutely essential, and problems will continue until we consciously recognize the source and discard it. It is in the dark night of the soul, between the falling apart and the rebuilding, the stages of discovery and recovery, that we will have identified that, not only are these old beliefs nonessential, but they are a direct impediment to growth.

You're Not Too Old!

Since we can count on better health due to medical advances and our own fitness regimen, deduct twenty years from your current chronological age (e.g., 50 – 20 = 30). Think what you would do with your life if you were twenty years younger, having the experience and knowledge you have now! Then strike out and do it! (Harkness 1999)

Self-defeating behavior might come from a self-concept based on low self-esteem. Two common behaviors are the drive for perfectionism (which stops us from making the decisions to start and learn along the way) and a heavy emphasis on material consciousness. Alice Walker commented, "We are living a meaningless culture . . . seeing progress as how much we can buy" (quoted in Thomas 2004, p. 5). These behaviors are closely tied to low self-esteem, and they create habitual anxiety and fear of risk and rejection. We must recognize and discard our self-defeating behaviors and modify perfectionism, procrastination, passivity, impulsiveness, and irrational beliefs about self and our needs as dictated by others. Rigidity, the need for tight control, lack of trust, pessimism, "yes, but . . . ," and giving our power away must all be jettisoned. Fear of the future, fear of failure, fear of success, fear of intimacy, fear of knowing, inertia—whatever binds you must be left behind. Collecting "mad dogs"—toxic people—lack of balance, workaholism, shame, guilt for wanting something different, aping our elders, regrets, confusing money with success, hopelessness, victim mentality, defensiveness, hostility, and aggression must be acknowledged and purged from our lives if we are to get to our authentic self and pursue our passionate purpose.

Give yourself permission to take chances. If a habit isn't working, try something new. When self-esteem and personal power are high, we seek success; when low, we seek to avoid failure. Activities 9 and 10 list typical self-defeating talk and behaviors. Use them to make an inventory of attitudes and thoughts to leave behind.

ACTIVITY 9: Self-Defeating Self-Talk

Do you find yourself anywhere in the following list of statements?

- *I am powerless.*
- *My background set me up to fail.*
- *I need to control my world or it will fly away.*

- *I don't have the capacity to cope.*

- *I am incapable.*

- *I'm not good enough.*

- *I'm obsessed with doing all things exactly right.*

- *I can't ask others for help.*

- *Trusting others is asking for trouble.*

- *I value security and avoid risk at all costs.*

- *I'm shy and don't relate well to others.*

- *I'm too old to make any changes.*

- *I avoid conflict at all costs.*

- *It's a dog-eat-dog world out there.*

- *I can't have a failure on my record.*

- *I'm really overqualified for my job.*

ACTIVITY 10: Identifying Your Self-Defeating Behaviors

Think through your chaos of change experience (personal and career), and identify examples of the following behaviors:

- *Doing the same thing repeatedly while hoping for different results*

- *Feeling continuing distrust and cynicism*

- *Postponing obvious and unaddressed issues*

- *Determined—manic—trying to be in control and make the old way work*

- *Running away to relieve pain on a temporary basis*

ACTIVITY 10 cont'd

- *Leaping quickly to a similar situation, which ultimately creates even more problems*

- *Feeling vulnerable and unconsciously setting oneself up for the problem to happen again*

- *Changing environments but still carrying negative feelings; earlier loss is still festering, not healing*

- *Taking self with you—recycling the same scenario but in a different setting*

- *Alternating between frenzy and paralysis: jumping from one state to another*

- *Running from hot to cold—vacillating, worrying, postponing, responding with "yes, but . . ."*

- *Experiencing delay and procrastination, wasting energy and resources, having anxiety, daydreaming, being indecisive*

- *Pounding on walls of self-made prison and collapsing helplessly into the role of victim*

- *Going to the door repeatedly, but never opening it and moving*

- *Ignoring or denying the necessity to take action to change*

- *Covering up—deadening oneself with drugs, food, alcohol, sex, shopping, workaholism*

- *Pretending there is no problem, hiding the negative from self and others*

- *Building iron fences—protective walls to conceal the problem*

- *Wearing a heavy mask, feeling like a fake, avoiding any concept of authentic self*

Fear of Failure

Our fear of failure opposes, dampens, and inhibits our ability to undertake achievement-oriented activities. Most frequently, fear doesn't motivate us toward constructive action; it paralyzes us. Fear is an increasing phenomenon that undermines the commitment, motivation, and confidence of people, especially in the workplace. People acting from fear are guarded, trying to impress others and protect themselves. Fear breeds inauthenticity, which eats away energy; it's simpler and takes less energy to be the real self. Activity 11 provides a questionnaire for discovering the fears that keep you from reaching your authentic self.

Learning About Failure from Michael Jordan

I have missed more than 9,000 shots in my career. I have lost almost 300 games. On 26 occasions, I have been entrusted to take the game-winning shot—and missed. And, I have failed over and over and over again in my life. And, that is why I succeed.

ACTIVITY 11: Resisting Change Questionnaire

Rank yourself from 1 to 10 (10 being the highest) on the following self-conversations. The higher the score, the more you resist change.

Fear of weakness: *I must shore up* all *talents.*

Fear of failure: *If I fail, what will they think of me?*

Fear of success: *If I succeed, what will they expect of me next?*

Fear of the future: *I want all information in order to gain total control*

ACTIVITY 11 cont'd

Fear of the unknown: *Who knows what may happen.*

Indecision/Procrastination: *I'll do it later, maybe.*

Denial: *I'm fine the way I am . . . but* you *could improve.*

Negativism: *I can't, so why try?*

Habit: *I've always been this way.*

Low self-esteem: *I simply can't succeed no matter what I try.*

Inconvenience: *I'd have to change my whole schedule.*

Uncertainty over the reward: *Is it worth it?*

Fear of looking silly: *What would I look like?*

Threat to security: *Will they still like me if I do better than they do?*

Real or imagined opposition: *My spouse/partner hasn't said, but I know he/she wouldn't like it.*

Double-bind syndrome: *Yes, but . . .*

MAKING DECISIONS WITH FORESIGHT

The aptitude of foresight is related to long-range personal planning, according to Irvin Shambaugh, coauthor of *You and Your Aptitudes* (1983), a publication of Aptitude Inventory Measurement Service (AIMS). Foresight is defined as an innate ability to produce alternate solutions to solve sudden problems that separate you from your goal: "Foresight seems to maintain and accomplish long range plans in their subconscious minds" (p. 154). Those with little foresight let difficulties rule their course of action. They change goals to overcome the difficulties instead of changing their actions. Strong foresight helps one to find ways around the obstacle to achieve goals. This is critical in career planning.

Foresight, according to Edward Cornish (2004), is "the ability to make decisions that are judged to be good not just in the present moment but in the long run" (p. 213). People with strong foresight can think ahead by intuitively identifying and assessing a variety of possibilities and making astute judgments about what will work. They can invent a number of ways to minimize the effects of wild cards and can turn disadvantage to advantage. Sometimes others mistake this for luck. The process outlined in Activity 12 will help you make decisions with foresight.

ACTIVITY 12: Decision-Making Outline

For each change you are contemplating, fill in the reasons for making or not making the change.

	Making the change	Not making the change
Benefits for self • *Immediate* • *Long-term*		
Negatives for self • *Immediate* • *Long-term*		
Benefits for others		
Negatives for others		
Self-esteem results		

MAINTAINING FOCUS

Maintaining focus is essential for moving from a vision to a goal. For some, a loose focus, direction, and action plan are essential to success, whereas for others, the opposite is necessary. For example, some people tend to be narrowly focused, one-dimensional, and very directed, and they have always known exactly what they were going to do in their career. Whether the career fit them was not necessarily the issue. They had a plan and were very goal oriented and stayed on track to achieve it.

However, since they are typically quite single-minded, when the planned goals aren't working for whatever reason—internal or external—they become almost totally directionless and suffer from severe tunnel vision. When the original plan is thwarted, they can't generate an alternative plan or direction. It's as if their entire future is cut off. They see no options and are at a loss for ideas. Never having thought in terms of alternatives, and unable to tolerate ambiguity, they have the tendency to grab the first thing they see available to them. Usually very result oriented, they feel better with a goal—even if it is not a good fit for their future—until it, too, is cut off.

It is necessary for people with a narrow focus to broaden their perspective about who they are, their potential options, their skills, and what their possibilities could be, then to provide related information on the world outside of their narrow sight lines. Gradually, once they begin to see viable options, they can begin to move forward in another career direction. However, they must become genuine seekers—open to new ideas—and must assume an inquisitive, exploratory thought process, taking a creative loosening-up approach.

There is another group of people who are quite different. They are exploring career redirection but have worked and dabbled for years in multiple activities in many different directions. They have experienced it all, or so it seems, and are brimming with multiple ideas and strategies. Frequently strong generalists and excellent communicators, they can jump into a new arena, become totally engrossed, work very hard and learn everything about it in a short while; but they can drop that and impulsively jump to something else without much forethought or planning when another interest grabs their attention.

Instead of bringing a narrow focus, as those in the first group do, they bring the whole universe and all kinds of possibilities with them. What is really staggering to them is that they have too many options and too many ideas, but no direction or focus on long-term goals. For many, the greatest fear is that if they make a strong, long-term commitment to succeed in one area, they will be forced to leave behind something they value. They feel they can't take everything with them if they become highly focused, and they may well be right.

Their nature is to get in the general stream of activities and leap on things as they move along. Sometimes, this works well and they may bump into the right career activity. However, this can be quite risky. As the opposite of the narrowly focused group, these people do not consciously plan, set goals, and take action. Happenstance, fate, or luck takes over. This more loosely focused group, at about age thirty-five or forty, begins to feel a need for more focus, for being recognized for being superb. Such people now want to have an impact and be an expert, to be known as being really good at something instead of a jack of all trades. Many feel that they are somehow missing something, that they have no solid area of expertise and lack depth. These adults need an entirely different approach for their career planning. They need a strong future vision and a written plan to achieve it, which they must keep before them daily.

ACTION STEPS

The establishment of a lofty goal or purpose in itself is not enough to develop solid achievement. Our mission and long-term goals must be redefined into concrete immediate and long-term action steps that we can attain mainly through our own efforts—without depending largely on actions by others—though we would be wise to connect and engage their support for information and contacts. To move forward in gaining our purpose we must have a future vision, which is based on the internal authentic self, our success criteria and Meaning Magnets, and the external research for matching career opportunities. This is all integrated into our career design plan, and we can then develop an action plan for moving forward.

To achieve our purpose, we must determine the first step, followed by or integrated with a second. We pay careful attention to the specific immediate actions to be taken. To worry about far distant difficulties (which can be the negative result of strong foresight) creates paralyzing anxiety. Answering the questions in Activity 13 will give you practice in acting on your goals.

ACTIVITY 13: Acting on Your Goals

Imagine you have just won the lottery.

- *What would you do the first six months?*

- *What goals would you act on over the long term?*

- *What can you begin to do now in small ways to move toward these goals without winning the lottery?*

The Paths of Action

While the path of action varies dramatically for each client, actions usually fall into one of four categories:

- *Enhancing and refocusing current career/job:* building personal and career competence, self-marketing, making contacts, making job proposals, becoming an intrapreneur inside the corporation

- *Finding a job:* a new job in the same field or (if a career change) in a new field, developing resumes, writing cover letters, making contacts, researching companies, honing interview skills, negotiating

- *Radical career change:* retraining and building specific skills through certification, degrees, internships, or focused volunteer activity

- *Starting or buying a business:* becoming an entrepreneur, a free agent, "Brand You, Inc.," a PIC (professional independent contractor/consultant), a freelancer, creating a business and marketing plan, and developing the financial and management know-how to succeed

Free Agent/Entrepreneur

Entrepreneurship isn't for everyone, though it is a growing need in our current era. People who do have entrepreneurial tendencies can either create a start-up or buy an existing business. Some can become intrapreneurs, effectively and strategically creating change within a large organization, or PICs, or free agents (as labeled by Daniel Pink, 2001), successfully offering contracting or professional services.

Many people take their creativity and their need for self-expression to the business world—and they must have the opportunity to use this creativity. Those who begin their own business from the initial start-up phase have a high creative need. The process of moving a business idea from initial concept through the beginning phases meets that need. Later, when the creating has ended and it is necessary to face the reality of day-to-day implementation and management (for which they may have scant interest and ability), some entrepreneurs want out. An entrepreneur who is interested only in the creating may be wise to sell that business and go start another.

Another option is to bring in an excellent manager and let that person take the business to the next level, but entrepreneurs frequently find it difficult or even impossible to turn over control to someone else.

Do you have what it takes to be an entrepreneur? Activity 14 will help you answer that question.

ACTIVITY 14: Free Agent/Entrepreneur Characteristics Indicator

Indicate how true the following statements are about you by assigning a number to each of the following statements
1=Not at all 2=Slightly 3=Somewhat 4=Quite well 5=Completely

- *Need to feel a strong sense of control over my own destiny*

- *Possess foresight and commitment to work toward long-term future goals*

- *Maintain firm belief in my ability to achieve my goals*

- *See myself as an "overcomer" with a high level of tenacity and determination*

- *Know how to build on successes and learn from failures*

- *Tolerate frustration and ambiguity*

- *Deal successfully with modest to high levels of uncertainty and job insecurity*

- *Have the knowledge and/or technical skills in my field for building a successful business*

- *Hold a healthy respect for managing projects, people, and money*

- *Have a close family member who has owned his/her own business*

- *Can visualize a purpose—a plan to create and implement*

Paul's Taking-Action Story

Paul had been a highly successful business student in accounting at the University of Indiana. He worked briefly as an accountant but found it boring. He then attended the University of Virginia Law School, but it didn't feel like a fit—too many blue bloods for his blue-collar comfort. Nor did he feel connected to the practice of law, though he succeeded in becoming a partner in a law firm dealing with real estate.

According to the Holland Assessment Theory, his interests were highly "enterprising" and "social," also with "artistic" surfacing, indicating a strong connection with people and business but in an innovative way. He carefully researched and rejected investment banking and venture capital and considered applying to Harvard for an MBA, which we decided was merely postponing the career focus.

He resigned from his position without an absolute plan of action and took a vacation—but was feeling a dark night. He had said that if he could come up with an entrepreneurial idea, he had a friend who would probably help finance it. At this point, synchronicity enters: Quite coincidentally, a friend of a client who was looking for a lawyer to help with an Internet business idea contacted me and I passed the referral on to Paul. It all fell into place.

Though Paul's knowledge of technology was zero and the decision was indeed "scary," he did not hesitate. He contacted his investment friend and another lawyer friend (also a former client—an excellent detailed hands-on manager).

In summary, their business built a new concept of broadcasting on the Internet, went public, and had an IPO of 249 percent the first day. Before the "bust," they sold the business for almost $6 billion, making instant millionaires of employees. After turning down the offer of COO at a major Internet company, Paul spent two years as a "social entrepreneur," developing an active foundation focusing on athletics and education for inner-city children and hands-on help for minority business start-ups. This social service orientation was shown to be strong in Paul's earlier assessment. Now following up on his creativity—another distinctive feature of his personality—he has entered the entertainment/film field, producing movies and purchasing theaters with the purpose of moving away from the traditional Hollywood model. "Just because something has been a certain way forever doesn't mean it's the best way" summarizes his purpose.

His message, which he generously shares with other CDA clients, is this:

- Know and follow your passion.
- Forget fear.
- Have a partner who brings what you don't have.
- Substance and sizzle are necessary for a successful business.
- Timing is critical.
- Keep control but build a team.

Figure 2 illustrates the four steps used to move through the career transition process. The first two steps, looking inward and looking outward, require much learning and research, and result in uncovering your Meaning Magnets and success criteria. The third step, looking forward, integrates and coordinates the insights from the first two steps to create a decision on a future image—a vision of the future. It is a destination to pursue with passion and direction for the long term. The action plan of the fourth step outlines the activities necessary to reach the future image.

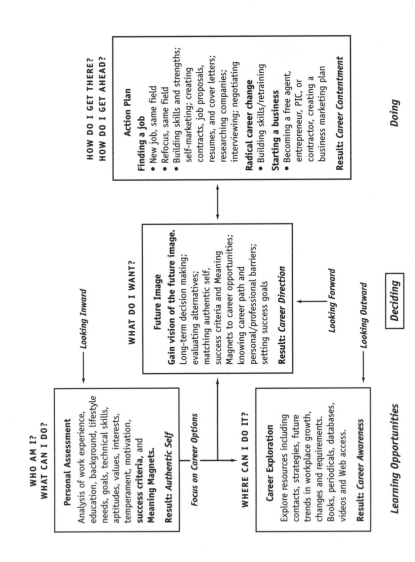

WHO AM I?
WHAT CAN I DO?

Personal Assessment

Analysis of work experience, education, background, lifestyle needs, goals, technical skills, aptitudes, values, interests, temperament, motivation, **success criteria,** and **Meaning Magnets.**

Result: *Authentic Self*

— *Looking Inward*

Focus on Career Options

WHAT DO I WANT?

Future Image
Gain vision of the future image.
Long-term decision making; evaluating alternatives; matching authentic self, success criteria and Meaning Magnets to career opportunities; knowing career path and personal/professional barriers; setting success goals

Result: *Career Direction*

— *Looking Forward*

WHERE CAN I DO IT?

Career Exploration

Explore resources including contacts, strategies, future trends in workplace growth, changes and requirements. Books, periodicals, databases, videos and Web access.

Result: *Career Awareness*

— *Looking Outward*

HOW DO I GET THERE?
HOW DO I GET AHEAD?

Action Plan

Finding a job
• New job, same field
• Refocus, same field
• Building skills and strengths; self-marketing; creating contracts, job proposals, resumes, and cover letters; researching companies; interviewing; negotiating

Radical career change
• Building skills/retraining

Starting a business
• Becoming a free agent, entrepreneur, PIC, or contractor, creating a business marketing plan

Result: *Career Contentment*

Doing

Learning Opportunities   Deciding

Figure 2—Creative Process for Taking Charge of Your Career

NINE

Looking Beyond

The most beautiful thing we can experience is the mysterious.
It is the source of all true art and science.

—ALBERT EINSTEIN

In this final chapter, we will take a brief look beyond the individual to chaos and change in organizations.

COMPETITION VERSUS COOPERATION IN ORGANIZATIONS

If complexity systems and business practices are more completely integrated, we can work more effectively within them and with deeper fulfillment. The core of the Darwinian theory of evolution, now under much questioning, is that individuals act in their own interests first and last. Bitter competition was considered the law of nature. Roger Lewin (1992), however, emphasizes that "in the new economy, strategy based on conventional competition and cooperation will give way to strategy based on co-evolution as companies adapt in concert" (p. 208).

While change is beginning, competition and survival of the fittest are still dominant in most organizations. Companies using competition only can certainly make advances, but this strategy is of limited long-term value. The "notion of competition as we know it should be allowed to die and be replaced by thinking more in terms of whole systems" (Lewin 1992, p. 209). According to Bruce Bower (1998, p. 205), new generations of economists and social scientists are discovering that people are in fact naturally inclined to cooperate for the common good. This certainly challenges the Darwinian assumptions that economic behavior is "rational" only if it is selfish and self-interested.

Dee Hock, founder and CEO emeritus of Visa, maintains that organizations are based on flawed seventeenth-century concepts that are no longer relevant to the vast systemic social and environmental problems we experience daily. In *Birth of a Chaordic Age* (1999), Hock delineates a path based on "chaordic" principles, which harmoniously blend *chaos and order, competition and cooperation.* He stresses that these are not contraries but are complementary: "One cannot exist without the other" (p. 263). In a chaordic age, we employ a clear sense of purpose and sound principles to quickly reach specific, short-term objectives, rather than longer-term, fixed objectives.

In a talk to would-be entrepreneurs (2003), Mort Meyerson said, "Order is a false god . . . chaos is wild and it's a goddess. We can talk about gods and evil, chaos and order, life and death, but we've got to have some of each."

John Hagel (1996) states that the Darwinian approach is of limited value in an increasingly high-tech world. "Webs emerge from the turmoil wrought by uncertainty and change. They spread risk, increase flexibility, enhance an industry's innovative capability and reduce complexity for individual participants. . . . The more companies—and customers—that join, the stronger the web becomes" (p. 6).

John Holland, labeled "Mr. Emergence" in Roger Lewin's 1992 book, said, "Reductionism has been tremendously powerful. You take a system, study the parts, and you can understand a lot about the system. But what complexity science says is that you have to look at the interactions as well as the parts" (p. 213). Interaction of the systems is the key.

TRADITIONAL BUSINESS MODELS ARE PASSÉ

In 1994, several McKinsey partners met in Paris to discuss the firm's business strategy consulting practice, and determined that most consulting approaches that were taught and used were outdated and inappropriate. Most companies assumed that with the right analysis, the future could be forecast with enough precision to identify the right strategy. But rapid changes and high levels of uncertainty were making this increasingly difficult. The McKinsey partners developed a team of sixty of their consultants, several academics, and a hundred companies on six continents to study strategy under high uncertainty resulting from rapid change. They determined that in choosing strategies under uncertainty, there is no easy answer, but the process is made harder when outdated approaches from predictable environments are used (Courtney, 2001).

In times of great uncertainty, the usual business process is marginally helpful at best and dangerous at worst. In their book *Embracing Uncertainty*, Phillip Clampitt and Robert DeKoch (2001) provide insight on the benefits of embracing uncertainty, offer reasons why people suppress uncertainty, explain myths that inhibit it, and give guidelines for embracing it. They suggest challenging existing rules and developing an aesthetic appreciation for chaotic environments. To catalyze action in uncertain times, they advise, look for deeper patterns, experiment, play the odds, and develop an integrated strategy.

Shoshana Zuboff (2004) asserts that our old capitalism is dead. She describes what is happening in this way: "A business model hits its stride, only to be overtaken by rigidity, resistance to changes and wasted interests. Its wealth-creating power and zest for innovation go into decline, and everyone is left to fight over a shrinking pie" (p. 97). However, society continues to evolve and people move on across a growing chasm, leaving old organizations behind and taking their marketplace of new needs with them. Zuboff coninues, "We are at this crossroads in business—a chasm of outrage and mistrust separates people and organizations."

CREATION OF A SUPPORT ECONOMY WITHIN THE ORGANIZATION

Lack of trust is a major trend. Zuboff (2004) cites a recent Harris Poll that found that only 4 percent of U.S. adults trust HMOs; 12 percent trust phone companies; 96 percent of employees want more flexibility and control over their time; and 73 percent are willing to curtail careers in favor of more family time. A 1997 Wharton Survey (see Koretz, 1997, p. 26) shows that 70 percent of U.S. companies are struggling with low morale and lack of trust, principally as a result of downsizing.

There is a new breed of people who are educated, informed, and connected—not content to be anonymous consumers and members of the masses. As employees, they are tired of stuffing their complex, individual lives into the simplistic career structures of most organizations. Zuboff (2004) is hearing, "We want more than just goods and services, paychecks and promotions. We want support in living our increasingly complex lives as we choose—'a support economy'" (p. 97).

Our former capitalism has had its day. Now it's a challenge to reinvent commerce for our times, and organizations need to be at the forefront of this reinvention. Companies are rooted in an inwardly focused business logic invented a century ago to deal with mass-manufactured goods for mass consumers. That logic emphasizes concentration, command and control, cost and efficiency. This type of managed capitalism was successful for decades, and capitalism is a renewable resource: New business models are invented to connect with people with unmet needs. Complexity is inching itself more and more into the new model.

MANAGERS MANAGING CHAOS

The hot new skill for leaders is the ability to manage chaos—culturally, structurally, and emotionally. Managers can be either stressed or energized by change. It's more difficult for those used to being given all their orders; 70 percent will need help. They must lead companies through today's chaos to create new ways of doing business, new ways of thinking, and new ways of managing people—a whole new corporate culture. They must embrace and participate in radical transformation, then make it happen. Believing in worker teams, customer focus, and employee empowerment is essential.

Rosabeth Moss Kanter, in *Best of Both Worlds* (1992), suggests that chaos may have a silver lining—creating new ways of organizing people, ideas, and whole corporations. However, change requires constant learning. To managers today, chaos is not just a scientific theory; it is a daily experience. Maintaining the same structure for long—let alone getting organized at all—can seem miraculous! Chaos abounds: Actions taken to solve one problem often create problems elsewhere.

Kanter (1992) labels management a balancing act—the juggling of contradictions to try to get the best of attractive but opposing alternatives. Order is a temporary illusion, strategy a moving target. "Leaders cannot impose authority on a world of constant motion; they can only hope to steer some of that action toward productive ends" (p. 9). But chaos need not mean action without guidance or limits. New organizational models offer the best of both worlds. It is not *either/or* but *both/and*—enough structure for continuity, but not so much that creative responses to chaos are stifled. We need both flexibility and direction, autonomy and authority.

Managing the "Measurable Middle"

The new law of management coined by Kanter (2001) is managing through the "miserable middle" (p. 128). According to this maxim, every new project, every new idea, runs into trouble before it reaches fruition. *Everything looks like a failure in the middle.* The vulnerability to failure increases with the number of ways the initiative differs from current approaches: the more innovation, the more problems. This applies directly to adults in career transition. I repeatedly stress the importance of realistic optimism, but also expect some miserable middle distress. Kanter lists four root causes:

- *Forecasts fall short.* Because it is difficult to predict how long a change will take or how much it will cost, delays are almost ensured. Project leaders must be prepared to secure additional resources, beg for additional time, or figure out creative ways to maximize scarce resources.

- *Unexpected obstacles pop up.* Every change creates unanticipated consequences. Teams must be prepared to respond, to troubleshoot, and to make adjustments. Without room to explore other approaches, the venture is doomed from the start.

- *Momentum slows.* Organizations typically hold exciting launches at the start and blow-out celebrations at the end but forget morale boosters in the middle--when problems are faced, multiple demands pile up, e-mails are not returned, and the team is weary.

- *Critics get louder.* Enter politics. Objectives pile up. The project is under assault. Powerful sponsors need to remind people of the vision and use their clout to neutralize the critics.

To manage the "miserable middles," managers should focus on cultivating the Type CC personality to be courageous and flexible. They should make sure the idea is still viable, keep selling, nurture their team and communicate, and celebrate each milestone.

Encouraging the Authentic Individual

Marcus Buckingham and Donald Coffman, in *First Break All the Rules* (1999), conclude that for talented employees to succeed, they need great managers—especially immediate supervisors who understand and remember that "each individual is true to their nature" (p. 57). They emphasize that managers can't totally remodel a subordinate, but must understand and capitalize on who they are by nature—their authentic selves. People don't change that much. Don't waste time trying to put in what was left out. Good managers do not help people fix their weaknesses. This is advice to remember: *Try to draw out what was left in!* Because talents are the driving force behind job performance, in turbulent times "the manager's role is to reach inside each employee and release his unique talents into performance" (p. 58).

Managing with Creativity and Intuition

Bill Lee, in *Mavericks in the Workplace* (1998), describes the thinking that stifles dynamic creativity in the business world. Today, a problem lands on a decision maker's desk; to handle it, he breaks it down into parts, classifies or pigeonholes them, and then solves each piece by applying the applicable theoretical tool. The problem can be labeled "a routine accounting problem" or "like a situation in another branch" to give it a familiar look. Such thinking, according to Lee, is "based on the dubious notion that unchanging principles underlie business, and that managers must seek out highly trained experts with elaborate theories to explain them" (p. 115). Lee stresses that breaking situations down into parts and applying the "correct" theory and then putting the pieces back into a whole doesn't work to reflect reality any more than does gluing together the pieces of a broken mirror.

Organizations in the throes of change often face challenging questions: What will the future look like, and what resources, human and capital, will be needed? How should they be organized and distributed? Authorities agree that the higher one goes in an organization, the greater the need for intuition. In spite of the elaborate personnel and organizational development programs implemented over the past decade, the productive use of human capital—particularly intuitive talent—remains a relatively primitive art, according to Weston Agor (1989, p. 20).

Highly intuitive managers tend to be most innovative and insightful in strategic planning and decision making, and also better at finding new ways of doing things or determining if a new product will fly. However, organizations often thwart or drive out this talent, so the talent they need most is suppressed or totally lost. Since higher-up managers tend to prefer people who think as they do, new ideas are usually not encouraged, and unconventional approaches to problem solving encounter enormous resistance. Every day intuitive people withdraw emotionally or leave the organization. Intuitive talent, with the commitment to experimentation rather than bureaucracy, may exist at all levels of an organization but may be dramatically underutilized.

Gary Klein (2003) recognizes serious barriers to intuitive decision making, such as organizational policies, rapid turnover, pace of change, procedures—playing it safe, and information technologies. He, along with others, warns that there are limits to intuitive decision making—complex and uncertain tasks make intuition hard to use. It doesn't work in gambling, because gambling is based on random fluctuation, not a predictable reality. He recommends that we start with intuition, not analysis—balance the two out, and don't agonize over a perfect choice. Most desperate appeals to intuition come when we are wrestling with uncertainty—all kinds of uncertainty. Klein maintains that those trained in creative problem solving enjoy it and don't dread creating the ideas for forward thinking. They can identify problems, and are not afraid to implement a plan. Confidence emerges: They don't wait for the problem to fully develop, but initiate intuitive perception of action to turn chaos into creativity. They can change chaos into consistency and cash.

EPILOGUE

*I say to you: we must still have chaos within us
to be able to give birth to a dancing star.*

—FRIEDRICH NIETZSCHE

Freedom is knowing our options; this is my mantra. I grew up with the West Virginia state motto, "Mountaineers are always free!" However, I also heard "freedom carries responsibility" from my family, and much was expected—because of our freedom to become. If we are to deal successfully with our future, we cannot huddle together in our known fears and frustrations. We must learn options, develop strategic plans, and move with courage beyond the comfort zone. With sound, planned, calculated, and educated risks we can escape our self-imposed prisons. Indeed, we can realize that failure is often the fee we pay to access new opportunities. However, we can control the cost of these failures.

Helping people gain a sense of freedom by realizing we have options in our work life is my mission, my passion—the driving motivational force in my personal and professional life. What do I mean by freedom—or the lack of it? We live in an increasingly complex world, and we see chaos and interpret it as decay and destruction. Millions feel powerless, directionless, cynical, victimized, depressed, and trapped. I talk daily with talented, successful adults who see themselves stalled in a meaningless, unchallenging, and sometimes even abusive work situation. They feel they have no choice but to stay put, regardless of the poor fit. After all, they selected this career path, it's paying their bills, and they should stick with it.

143

Imprisoned in a vicious cycle by what we see as our material needs, we spend money to fill an empty hole in our gut because there is little other purpose in our lives. Many are burned out and sense that their work life is out of control. We long for something different, better—but we can't name it, can't find it, or suspect we wouldn't recognize it if we ran into it; if we did find it, we might be too fearful of the risk involved to take it. "I'm looking for the second half of my life. I could get it, if I just knew what it was!" The successful executive who told me this echoed what I hear from many clients seeking their career options.

Our work can be a cry of disappointment or the stirring call of a new purpose. The discoveries that accompany a career transformation on the edge of chaos are like a compass. Discovering a meaningful purpose and direction strengthens the will and resolve to bring work into alignment with belief—the head with the heart. We gain a new respect for the characteristics of the new science of chaos and complexity by increasing our intuition, our creativity, our connection with others, our calculated risk taking. We realize that security, in the conventional sense, is an illusion, and that success itself must be redefined.

A NEW FRONTIER

What I urge my clients in pursuit of purpose to realize and remember always is that today we are pioneers on a new frontier. We distance ourselves from the familiar and head toward the unknown and the unnamed. While this is fearful, it's a challenge and an opportunity to be a modern pathfinder, creating new routes and directions for ourselves and others to follow us.

The colliding and overlapping of the old age and the new age, of being "here or there" (but maybe both in a single lifetime), has created a breakdown in our expectations for the ways things are supposed to be. The loss of myth, assumptions, and rules has created great anxiety, doubt, and extreme uncertainty about the way the world works, the way it is supposed to work, and the way we want it to work. The effect is that millions are unaware or heedless that the former dependable rules or truths we consciously or subconsciously use are now just half-truths that set us up for failure or only limited success in our lives and careers.

Mindlessly following the rules of the past has the potential to seriously impact if not permanently stall our career success and personal growth. Like many Americans, most of my clients with serious career problems have done all the right things for success and are dressed up with the proper academic credentials, sophisticated work experience, and high expectations, but they are stuck, lacking the focus and direction or, in some cases, the initiative to take creative charge of their careers.

Something isn't working. "Is this all there is? This isn't the way things are supposed to be!" is the muffled roar from millions. In *Cry for Myth* (1991), Rollo May calls this our cry for a collective myth that would help us make sense in a senseless world and would give us a fixed spot in a chaotic universe.

Today many highly talented adults are searching for direction, purpose, and meaning in their lives, a fixed spot they can accept and understand. May (1991) says that while the twentieth century was to be the age of enlightenment, "People are more confused, lacking in moral ideals, dreading the future, uncertain what to do to change things or how to rescue their own inner life" (p. 22).

DEALING WITH PARADOX

Our current "betwixt and between" era creates countless paradoxes, mind messages that are confusing and frustrating. Charles Handy (1994) says that living with paradox is like riding a seesaw. If you and the person on the other end know how the process works, it can be exhilarating. If the person on the opposite end forgets or neglects you, you can be in for a shock.

We crave clear-cut causes and effects in a world in which reality offers no assurance, where bad things can happen to good people for no identifiable or preventable reason. In ages past, such powerlessness and vulnerability were considered the work of vengeful gods with no sensitivity to human needs, but at least they could be held responsible.

Paradoxes are inevitable, and the more turbulent the times and the more complex the world, the more paradoxes there are (Handy, 1994, p. 12). We can learn to deal with conflicting, mixed messages, but they won't disappear. Developing the Type CC personality is essential in dealing with contradiction and uncertainty, ambiguity, paradox. Black-and-white, either/or answers and neat boxes seldom exist in complex times. We need to weigh and balance the types of paradoxes I have identified in the following list. These are the kinds of challenges we confront today.

- We face the highest unemployment rate in thirty years, yet future severe labor shortages are predicted.
- We define success in terms of money and status, but we feel guilty about it.
- Autonomy, choices, and options create "decidophia."
- We accumulate more degrees but know fewer career options.
- We crave freedom and autonomy but fear responsibility.
- We need to know but fear knowing.
- A strength carried to the extreme is a major weakness.
- If you have no weakness, you have no strengths—therefore you're mediocre.
- In rejecting your weaknesses, you cancel your strengths.
- You don't have to change *by* yourself but you must *do it* yourself.
- Positive transformation and rebirth are preceded by the pain of the dark night.

- Information overload creates information starvation.

- Be autonomous and self-reliant, but conform to the team.

- Be independent, but connect and collaborate with others.

- Be headstrong but heart wise.

- Gain external status, but base it on internal meaning and values.

- Keep your head in the clouds but your feet on the ground.

- Be loyal to the organization, but mind your own career.

- Death of custom can bring birth of self.

- We communicate worldwide via the Internet but never speak to the people next door.

- Sharpen your "crap detector," but practice positive resilience.

- Creativity and common sense are directly connected for success.

- Rigid focus on making a living wipes out making a life.

With all these contradictions and paradoxes, if we drop the fear of failure, we are free to develop wisdom and trust in ourselves. John Gardner (1990) summarizes the two seemingly contradictory ingredients that are at the heart of sustained morale and motivation:

- Positive attitudes toward the future and toward what can be accomplished through one's own intentional acts; and

- Accepting and recognizing that life is not easy and that nothing is ever finally safe.

Refocusing a career in this chaotic time is an internal and external process, requiring both conceptual and creative skills, as well as the ability to be specific, pragmatic, and action oriented. I ask the following four questions to anyone preparing to undertake this process of achieving meaning and money:

1. What does the world need now and in the future?

2. Do I have or can I get the skills to meet that need?

3. Would I value and find meaning and purpose in doing that?

4. Can I make a living doing that?

Conventional goals of success are like a blueprint drawn up by an architect who does not yet know the terrain and who has outlined a structure too rigid for nature. The purpose we have visualized and are pursuing is more the quality of an inner summons to move in a particular direction, feeling our way. It's a vision that can be realized in many ways.

THE STORY OF THE SWINGING BRIDGE

The thought of fleeing from fear to freedom and fun reminds me of when I was a very young child. I loved to go with my older brothers and sisters to visit my father's logging camp high in the mountains of West Virginia. Since there were no TVs or radios, my siblings and I provided a diversion for the dozens of loggers lonely for their families. They gave me much recognition for my verbal performances and also told me great stories. Unfortunately, the problem was getting to the camp. It was the biggest fear of my life.

We would first go by car to the railroad, catch a log train, and later get off and walk for what seemed forever, almost straight up a mountain. All too quickly we would come to my waking nightmare, the swinging bridge. High and loosely constructed, the bridge connected the two banks of a deep river. I was never physically adventurous, and my heart would sink! Even the Grand Canyon doesn't seem as deep or as wide to me today. An adult could not carry me across. I had to walk it alone. The bridge (or lack of a bridge) frightened and frustrated me. It had no firm structure, no secure sides, only a rope to hold and no other support—or so it seemed to me.

As if I were dancing, I had to walk with the rhythm of the bridge as it swung from side to side with each step I took. As I recall, once I started there was no turning back in panic. I am not certain whether the "no turning back" was a function of the bridge itself or if it was a rule designed by my older siblings to help me conquer the fear. Walking across that unpredictable and risky swinging bridge represented the greatest fear and challenge of my childhood. Yet, I had no choice if I wanted the fun and freedom of being on the other side, so I ventured forth at every opportunity.

So it is with millions of us in the first decade of this century. We must move successfully and with purpose and direction through this time of the swinging bridge, this age of uncertainty and unpredictability, though we may feel rootless and without moorings. Perhaps constantly tempted, we cannot, except in nostalgia, turn around; the safety of the former age as we remembered it no longer exists. At the same time, there may be little certainty that where we are headed is where we want to go, if we have any choice. After all, it's unknown and unfamiliar territory. We've never been there!

RESOURCES

Bronson, Po. "What Should I Do with My Life? The Real Meaning of Success and How to Find It." *Fast Company* (January 2003).

———. *What Should I Do With My Life?* New York: Random House, 2003.

Buckingham, Marcus, and Donald O. Clifton. *Now Discover Your Strengths.* New York: Free Press, 2001.

Cohen, Gene D. *The Creative Age: Awakening Human Potential in the Second Half of Life.* New York: Quill-HarperCollins, 2000.

Cox, W. Michael, and Richard Alm. *Myths of Rich and Poor: Why We're Better Off Than We Think.* New York: Basic Books, 2000.

Drucker, Peter. "The Shape of Things to Come." *Leader to Leader* (Summer 1996): 12–18.

Florida, Richard. *The Rise of the Creative Class: And How It's Transforming Work, Leisure, Community and Everyday Life.* New York: Basic Books, 2002.

Freedman, David H. "Is Management Still a Science?" *Harvard Business Review* (November–December 1992): 26–38.

Gladwell, Malcolm. *Blink: The Power of Thinking Without Thinking.* New York: Little, Brown, 2005.

Gleick, James. *Chaos: Making a New Science.* New York: Viking Press, 1987.

Hall, Cheryl. "Author in Search of 'Hyper.'" *Dallas Morning News,* November 21, 2003.

———. "Finding That Labor of Love," *Dallas Morning News,* July 11, 2004.

Hankin, Paul, Amory Lovins, and L. Hunter Lovins. *Natural Capitalism: Creating the Next Industrial Revolution.* Snowmass, Colo.: Rocky Mountain Institute, 2003.

Hawking, Stephen, ed. *On the Shoulders of Saints: The Great Works of Physics and Astronomy.* Philadelphia: Running Press, 2002.

May, Rollo. *Man's Search for Himself.* New York: W. W. Norton, 1953.

———. *The Courage to Create.* New York: Bantam Books, 1975.

Popcorn, Faith, and Lys Marigold. *Clicking: Sixteen Trends to Future Fit Your Life, Your Work and Your Business.* New York: HarperCollins, 1996.

Prigogine, Ilya. *Order Out of Chaos: Man's New Dialogue with Nature.* New York: Bantam Books, 1984.

———. *The End of Certainty.* New York: Free Press, 1996.

Seligman, Martin E. P. *Authentic Happiness*. New York: Free Press, 2002.

Siegfried, Tom. *The Bit and the Pendulum: From Quantum Computing to M Theory: The Physics of Information*. New York: Wiley, 2000.

Tawber, Gary, and Gayle Golden. "The Order of Chaos: In Unraveling the Mysteries of Disorder, Scientists Find Methods to the Madness." *Dallas Morning News*, September 3, 1984.

Waldrop, M. M. *Complexity: The Emerging Science at the Edge of Order and Chaos*. New York: Simon & Schuster, 1992.

Wheatley, Margaret J., and Myron Kellner-Rogers. *A Simpler Way*. San Francisco: Berrett-Koehler, 1996.

Wilber, Ken. *Quantum Questions: Mystical Writings of the World's Greatest Physicists*. Boulder: New Science Library, 1984.

REFERENCES

Agor, Weston H. "Intuition and Strategic Planning." *Futurist* (November–December 1989): 20–22.

Anderson, Harold H., ed. *Creativity and Its Cultivation*. New York: Harper & Row, 1959.

Arlington Institute. *Future Newsletter* (March 2, 2004): 13.

Assagioli, Robert. *Psychosynthesis*. New York: Esalen Publishing, Viking Press, 1965.

———. *The Act of Will*. New York: Penguin Books, 1973.

Barabási, Albert-László. *Linked: The New Science of Networks*. Cambridge, Mass.: Perseus, 2002.

Barker, Joel. *Discovering the Future: The Business of Paradigms* (film). Burnsville, Minn.: ChartHouse, 1996.

Bly, Robert. *A Little Book on the Human Shadow*. Ed. W. Booth. San Francisco: HarperSanFrancisco. 1988.

Bonabean, Eric. "Don't Trust Your Gut." *Harvard Business Review* (May 2003).

Bower, Bruce. "Yours, Mine and Ours." *Science News* 153, no. 3 (March 28, 1998): 205–207.

Briggs, John, and F. David Peat. *Seven Life Lessons of Chaos: Timeless Wisdom from the Science of Change*. New York: HarperCollins, 1999.

Buckingham, Marcus, and Curt Coffman. *First Break All the Rules*. New York: Simon & Schuster, 1999.

Campbell, Joseph. *The Power of Myth*. New York: Doubleday, 1988.

Carroll, Lewis. *Alice in Wonderland*. Grossett & Dunlap, 1946.

Childre, Doc, and Bruce Cryer. *From Chaos to Coherence: The Power to Change Performance*. Boulder Creek, Calif.: HeartMath, 2000.

Clampitt, Phillip G., and Robert J. Dekoch. *Embracing Uncertainty*. Armonk, N.Y.: M. E. Sharpe, 2001.

Cohen, Alan H. *Why Your Life Sucks and What You Can Do About It*. San Diego: Jodere Group, 2002.

Cornish, Edward. *Futuring: The Exploration of the Future*. Bethesda, Md.: World Future Society, 2004.

Courtney, Hugh. *20/20 Foresight: Crafting Strategies in an Uncertain World*. Boston: Harvard Business School Press, 2001.

Dante, Alighieri. *The Inferno of Dante.* Trans. Robert Pinsky. New York: Farrar, Strauss & Giroux, 1994.

Devereaux, Mary O'Hara. Presentation given to the World Future Society. San Jose, Calif., 1994.

Devereaux, Mary O'Hara, and Robert Johnson. *Global Work: Bridging Distance, Culture and Time.* San Francisco: Jossey-Bass, 1994.

Dyson, Esther. *Release 2.0: A Design for Living in the Digital Age.* New York: Broadway, 1997.

Eldredge, John. *Wild at Heart: Discovering the Secret of a Man's Soul.* Nashville, Tenn.: Thomas Nelson, 2001.

Elgin, Duane. *Promise Ahead.* New York: Quill, HarperCollins, 2000.

Finari, Paul. *Understanding Systems Thinking, or a New Way of Understanding How the World Works.* Coquitlam, B.C.: Pacific Institute for Advanced Study, 2003.

Frankl, Viktor E. *Man's Search for Meaning: An Introduction to Logotherapy.* New York: Washington Square Press, 1959, 1963.

Gardner, Howard. *Frames of Mind: The Theory of Multiple Intelligences.* New York: Basic Books, 1983.

————. *Multiple Intelligences: The Theory in Practice.* New York: Basic Books, 1993.

Gore, Al. *Earth in the Balance: Ecology and the Human Spirit.* New York: Houghton Mifflin, 1992.

Grove, Andrew. *Only the Paranoid Survive.* New York: Currency Doubleday, 1997.

Hagel, John. "Spider vs. Spider." *McKinney Quarterly* no. 1 (1996): 6.

Handy, Charles. *The Age of Paradox.* Boston: Harvard Business School Press, 1994.

Harkness, Helen. *The Career Chase: Taking Creative Control in a Chaotic Age.* Mountain View, Calif.: Davies-Black Publishing, 1997.

————. *Don't Stop the Career Clock: Rejecting the Myths of Aging for a New Way to Work in the 21st Century.* Mountain View, Calif.: Davies-Black Publishing, 1999.

Harpur, Patrick. *The Philosophers' Secret Fire: A History of the Imagination.* Chicago: Ivan R. Dee, 2002.

Hillman, James. *Anima: An Anatomy of a Personified Notion.* Dallas: Spring Publications, 1985.

Hock, Dee. *Birth of the Chaordic Age.* San Francisco: Berrett-Koehler, 1999.

Holland, John H. *Discovering Career Options* (film). Career Design Associates, 1987.

Huey, John. "Managing in the Midst of Chaos." *Fortune* (April 5, 1993): 38.

Jacques, Elliott. "Death and the Midlife Crisis." *International Journal of Psychoanalysis* no. 46 (1965): 502–514.

James, William. *The Varieties of Religious Experience: A Study in Human Nature.* New York: Modern Library, 1902.

Jourard, Sidney M. *The Transparent Self.* New York: Van Nostrand Reinhold, 1971.

Jung, Carl Gustav. *The Undiscovered Self.* New York: New American Library, 1957.

Kanter, Rosabeth Moss. "The Best of Both Worlds." *Harvard Business Review* (November–December 1992): 9.

———. "Managing Through the Miserable Middle." *Business 2.0* 2, no. 9 (November 2001): 128.

Karpinski, Gloria D. *Where Two Worlds Touch: Spiritual Rites of Passage.* New York: Ballantine Books, 1990.

Kelly, Kevin. *Out of Control: The Rise of Neo-Biological Civilization.* Reading, Mass.: Addison-Wesley, 1994.

Klein, Gary. *Intuition at Work.* New York: Doubleday, 2003.

Koretz, G. "The Downside of Downsizing." *Business Week* (April 28, 1997): 26.

Lee, William G. *Mavericks in the Workplace: Harnessing the Genius of American Workers.* New York: Oxford University Press, 1998.

Lewin, Roger. *Complexity: Life at the Edge of Chaos.* New York: Macmillan, 1992.

Lewin, Roger, and Birute Regine. *The Soul at Work: Embracing the Power of Complexity Science for Business Success.* New York: Simon & Schuster, 2000.

Lifton, Robert J. *The Protean Self: Human Resilience in an Age of Fragmentation.* Chicago: University of Chicago Press, 1993.

Lorenz, Edward N. "Deterministic Non-Periodic Flow." *Journal of Atmospheric Science* (1963): 20, 130–141.

———. "Predictability: Does the Flap of a Butterfly's Wings in Brazil Set Off a Tornado in Texas?" *American Association for the Advancement of Science,* December 29, 1979.

Masterson, James F. *The Search for the Real Self: Unmasking the Personality Disorder of Our Age.* New York: Free Press, 1988.

May, Rollo. *Cry for Myth.* New York: W. W. Norton, 1991.

McLeish, John A. B. *The Ulyssean Adult.* Toronto: McGraw-Hill Ryerson, 1976.

Meyerson, Mort. "Everything I Know About Leadership Is Wrong." *Fast Company* supplement: "New Rules of Business" (1996): 6.

———. Keynote address at Southwest Equity Capital Summit. Dallas, October 22, 2003.

Michalko, Michael. "From Bright Ideas to Right Ideas: Capturing the Creative Spirit." *Futurist* (September–October 2003): 52–56.

Moore, Thomas. *Care of the Soul.* New York: HarperCollins, 1992.

Moyers, Bill. *A World of Ideas.* Ed. Betty Sue Flowers. New York: Doubleday, 1989 (Part 1), 1990 (Part 2).

Palmer, Parker J. *Let Your Life Speak.* San Francisco: Jossey-Bass, 2000.

Patterson, Karen. "Depression Reach Profound." *Dallas Morning News,* June 18, 2003.

Peters, Tom. *Re-Imagine! Business Excellence in a Disruptive Age.* London: Darling Kindersley, 2003.

———. *Brand Everything: Lessons in Leadership.* Wyncom.

Pink, Daniel. *Free Agent Nation.* New York: Warner Books, 2001.

———. "How to Make Your Luck." *Fast Company* (July 2003): 79.

Plato. *The Republic.* Trans. Allan Bloom. New York: Basic Books, 1968.

Ray, Michael, and Rochelle Myers. *Creativity in Business.* New York: Doubleday, 1989.

Senge, Peter. *The Fifth Discipline: The Art and Practice of the Learning Organization.* New York: Doubleday, 1990.

Shambaugh, Irvin C., Brenda Smith, and John Gaston. *You and Your Aptitudes.* Dallas: Aptitude Inventory Measurement Service (AIMS), 1983.

Siegel, Bernie. *Love, Medicine and Miracles.* New York: HarperCollins, 1986.

Smith, Emily. "Are You Creative?" *Business Week* (September 30, 1985): 80–84.

Stacey, Ralph D. *Complexity and Creativity in Organization.* San Francisco: Berrett-Koehler, 1996.

Stewart, Thomas. "How to Think with Your Gut." *Business 2.0* (November 2002): 98–104.

Sussman, Linda. *Speech of the Grail: A Journey Toward Speaking That Heals and Transforms.* Hudson, N.Y.: Lindisfarne Press, 1995.

Taylor, Frederick W. *Principles of Scientific Management.* New York: Harper & Row, 1911.

Thomas, Karen M. "You Have to Be of the Heart and Spirit." *Dallas Morning News,* May 24, 2004.

Thurow, L. C. *The Future of Capitalism.* New York: Morrow, 1996.

Useem, Michael. "Clear and Present Danger." *Fast Company* (July 2003): 29–30.

Viscott, David. *The Language of Feelings.* New York: Pocket Books, 1976.

Warren, Rick. *The Purpose Driven Life: What on Earth Am I Here For?* Grand Rapids, Mich.: Zondervan, 2002.

Wheatley, Margaret J. *Leadership and the New Science: Learning About Organization from an Orderly Universe.* San Francisco: Berrett-Koehler, 1994.

"Why Willie Loman Lives." *Economist,* June 19, 1999, p. 28.

Wiseman, Richard. *The Luck Factor: Changing Your Luck, Changing Your Life.* New York: Miramax, 2003.

Wordsworth, William. *William Wordsworth: The Major Works.* Oxford University Press, 2000.

Zuboff, Shoshana. "Evolving Insights." *Fast Company* (January 2004): 97.

INDEX